ABOUT *MORE DISCIPLES*

"In *More Disciples*, Doug Lucas examines a broad range of movements that multiply disciples and churches. He identifies the common principles and the variety of methods. The book is comprehensive and points the way to further learning. A great reference."

—**Steve Addison**, author of *Pioneering Movements: Leadership that Multiplies Disciples and Churches.*

"*More Disciples* ... establishes the global need for better disciple-making. It challenged me to get engaged. The book is filled with practical, proven concepts, approaches, and tools to get started and stay focused on disciple-making, including use of the Zume Project resources. I am looking forward to getting involved in a Zume small group and putting these principles into action."

—**Jerry Anderson**, elder (on sabbatical), Sunday School class teacher, and Zúme group facilitator, Northeast Christian Church, Louisville, KY

"You can make disciples, baptize, help people remember Jesus Christ through starting other groups of disciples and teaching them to do the same. ... Do not be dissuaded that you are not competent enough. Read *More Disciples* and press forward to finish the work Jesus Himself started - that the whole earth will be filled with the knowledge of the glory of God as the waters cover the sea (Hab. 2:14)."

—**Ian Benson,** Secretary, International Missionary Training Network, World Evangelical Alliance Mission Commission, www.theimtn.org

"In Jesus' priestly prayer in John 17:20, we see that the expectation of our Lord was disciples making disciples, 'I do not ask for these only but also for those who will believe through their word.' In *More Disciples*,

Doug Lucas reminds us that this is still the expectation of our Lord in the 21st century. It has always been God's plan to extend and expand His kingdom through simple men and women who love God with all their heart, soul and mind, who are obedient to Christ, and who are committed to pushing back darkness through multiplying disciples. *More Disciples* provides timeless principles and simple tools for those who desire to be a part of kingdom expansion."

—**R. Bruce Carlton**, Professor of Cross-Cultural Ministry, Oklahoma Baptist University; and author of Strategy Coordinator: Changing the Course of Southern Baptist Missions and Amazing Grace: Lessons on Church-Planting Movements from Cambodia

"The theme of modern missions is fast shifting away from adding new believers one by one to making disciples who multiply over and over again. If that is what you want to be a part of, then *More Disciples* will give you the tools you need to get started. Doug Lucas has given us a compass to chart the course, a clear track to run on and an inspiring glimpse of the Kingdom impact ahead for all who focus on *More Disciples* as their destination."

—**Harry Brown,** President, New Generations, formerly known as CityTeam International

"*More Disciples* is a must-read for every Christian! Making more disciples is the mission that Jesus left us with and should be a major focus of our lives. Doug does a great job articulating how every Christian can be a fruitful disciple-maker. Perhaps you question if God really can use you to make more disciples. Perhaps you assume that only pastors and missionaries can make more disciples. That couldn't be further from the truth. This book will set you on fire as you realize that God not only CAN use you but WANTS to use you to make many more disciples!"

—**Chris Galanos**, author of *From Megachurch to Multiplication: A Church's Journey Toward Movement,* and Founding and Lead Pastor of Experience Life Church in Lubbock, Texas, named by *Outreach Magazine* as one of the "Top 100 Fastest-Growing Churches."

front of me." Third, and finally, because as the primary vision-caster for one of the most effective sending agencies in the US, Doug's grasp of what is happening globally will inspire and challenge you to look again at the Great Commission. He'll give you a look that will cut through the centuries of tradition to a simple repeatable process that has the potential of the good news going viral. So please... Stop reading this endorsement right now and get into this book. I promise you, you will think and act differently about the Kingdom."

—**Roy Moran**, author of Spent Matches and Primary Cultural Architect of Shoal Creek Community Church, Chairman of the Board of "New Generations" and "Beyond."

"The tools and concepts in this book provide ways for us to be intentional in listening to God, pursuing the life He intends for us, knowing Him more deeply, making Him known more effectively, and, most importantly, loving Him more passionately. It provides a toolkit to help us build in this way. May you become a skilled craftsman."

—**Curtis Sergeant**, Founder of MetaCamp, content creator of the Zume course, and a trainer in disciple-making movements

"*More Disciples* is an important resource for facilitating the immergence of the next wave of multiplying discipleship practitioners. Doug Lucas shows why many have changed their ministry paradigm for the sake of kingdom expansion and why many others should consider doing so. *More Disciples* reminds those who already practice CPM/DMM principles to stay the course and to use this helpful resource to cast their disciple-making vision to others."

—**Mike Shipman**, author of *Any-3: Anyone, Anywhere, Anytime – Win Muslims to Christ Now!*

"We envision a world on fire for God, consumed with discipleship groups making discipleship groups that resemble the wild bush fires that consume vast lands in West Africa at the end of the rainy season.

Everywhere disciples go implementing the tools mentioned in *More Disciples*, bush fires will result that will consume the whole world with knowledge of the glory of God. Our passion is that we see the great commission finished in our lifetimes and we believe the practices mentioned in this book will make it possible for all the peoples of the earth to praise him. Praise God that he has allowed us to witness what he is doing to make disciples of all nations with our own eyes.

—**Terry and Amy** (last name held for security's sake), implementers of these strategies and life practices in West Africa.

"Multiplying movements of new disciples are transforming Asia, Latin America and Africa. Doug Lucas has written to help us in America experience the same joy, fulfillment, and spiritual fruitfulness. Doug traces history, explains process, and carefully details methodologies globally blessed. No longer do believers have to say, 'Why are we not seeing spiritual fruit like we read about in the New Testament and hear about overseas?' Doug is an experienced overseas missionary and agency administrator, but, more importantly in 2018, a hands on practitioner in the USA. He writes with passion, freely quoting from other practitioners such as Curtis Sergeant. He recommends a well-researched process built on solid Biblical principles supported by excellent online resources. As something like a great grandfather of many overseas movements cited in this book, I take special pleasure in recommending this simple practical handbook for every believer to multiply disciples."

—**Bill Smith**, Trainer, encourager, and prayer partner of many God uses to birth Church Planting Movements.)

"*More Disciples* is truly an excellent resource for people wanting to get started, or get better at, catalyzing multiplying disciples. But it will also be a very useful reference resource for CPM/DMM veterans. Doug is the president of a large American agency that has achieved remarkable breakthroughs in transitioning its teams to successfully catalyze movements. From that experience, Doug has distilled for us the processes that took him years to learn and apply. *More Disciples* is a handbook of practical knowledge that will enlighten the reader with rich insights and provide simple case studies along with many useful visuals. This is a timely, and much needed resource!

—**Jerry Trousdale**, Director of International Ministries, New Generations, and author of *Kingdom Unleashed: How Jesus' 1st-Century Kingdom Values Are Transforming Thousands of Cultures and Awakening His Church* and *Miraculous Movements: How Hundreds of Thousands of Muslims Are Falling in Love with Jesus.*

More Disciples is a book well done being published at a critical moment for the church and those who wish to see all nations as brothers in Christ. There are several major take-aways that will touch every audience. First, we applaud the emphasis on the fact that disciple-making movements begin in the hearts of those called to be disciple-makers. (Personally, I think we should never actually have to use the term disciple-maker, because the nature of a true disciple is to make more disciples.) Second, we love the link that *More Disciples* makes between disciple-making movements and churches. Personnel and resources, as well as doctrinal audits are the purview of the church; and disciple-making movements cannot reach maturity without the churches who support and foster movements. Finally, *More Disciples* addresses one of the weaknesses in disciple-making movements by supplying curricula that is culturally adaptive and ready for those who are interested. We're grateful for the hard work accomplished by the *More Disciples* team and I pray it blesses many practitioners so that even more movements will be started.

—**David Watson**, *Co-Author of Contagious Disciple Making: Leading Others on a Journey of Discovery*

A Guide to Becoming and
Multiplying Followers of Jesus

MORE
DISCIPLES

Doug Lucas
Foreword by David Garrison
Introduction and Epilogue by Curtis Sergeant

Cover design by Tina McCormick.
Unless indicated otherwise, all Scripture quotations in this publication
are from the HOLY BIBLE, NEW INTERNATIONAL VERSION˚ Copyright
© 1973, 1978, 1984 by International Bible Society. All rights reserved.

Revised First Edition

ISBN: 978-1-939124-16-6

Interior design by booknook.biz

ACKNOWLEDGMENTS

Thanks to all the Zúme Development team for inviting me to ride the wave with you, for your months of devotion to a dream that God's people can and should multiply, and for using your creative abilities for Kingdom good. Thanks, too, for permission to include so much of Zúme in this book.

Thanks to Frank Schattner for investing in our leadership back in summer of 2009 to help us start to digest all this and for introducing us to Curtis Sergeant, David Garrison, Steve P, Jeff A, Bruce Carlton, and Andy Smith. You trusted in us, believed in us, and encouraged us,

Thanks especially to Eric D. for bringing CPM/DMM practices to Team Expansion in 2009 and for being patient as I figured out its impact on me.

Thanks to Curtis Sergeant for his inspiration, his knowledge, his training, and for writing the Introduction, the Epilogue, and several other excerpts of this book. Thanks, too, for your suggestions for improvement.

I'm grateful to Rex & Janet Britton, Teresa B., Eric D., Linda E., Ryan F., Allan W., Jerry Anderson, and Penny Lucas for giving input and for helping check for typos. I'm especially grateful for Betty B., who invested day after day combing through this manuscript, proofing it one line at a time. This book is better because of her friendship and devotion to excellence.

Special thanks to Tina McCormick for endless hours of reading, editing, revising, and researching. It's obvious that the Great Commission is a passion for her.

Thanks to Penny Lucas for putting up with my zany work schedule and for being such a faithful friend and partner since 1979. And thanks to Chris and Caleb for being zany themselves and for encouraging me onward.

Most of all, **thanks to God for His abundant grace and mercy.**

Special note from the author and publisher: After covering expenses, all proceeds from the sale of this book will be applied toward the costs of translating the Zúme course into additional languages (as this book goes to print, 36 languages are in process; each language costs an additional $7500 to produce, on average) and conducting "live" DMM trainings in new locations worldwide.

CONTENTS

FOREWORD

By David Garrison

For as long as I have known him, Doug Lucas has been a servant leader of the Body of Christ in the pursuit of the Great Commission. This book is the culmination of a lifetime of humbly loving, serving, and leading us to do what Christ commanded two millennia ago: disciple the nations!

More Disciples addresses head on the fundamental question: What's it going to take to bring the world to faith and discipleship in Jesus Christ? From this clarion call to make disciples, we learn what it means to be a disciple and then move on to the question of "How?" *More Disciples* takes the centuries-old-challenge and, through the grace of God, places it within our grasp.

As a diligent student of the best practices in global missions, Lucas has compiled, sifted, and integrated the most fruitful mission practices from around the world and offered these up as a gift to anyone who wishes to see Christ's Great Commission mandate fulfilled.

The Great Commission was never meant to be limited to a vision statement or a frothy aspiration. Jesus meant for His disciples to do for the world what He had done for them: reproduce the life-transforming power of the gospel virally to the very ends of the earth.

As the Body of Christ, the Great Commission is neither a simple Messianic benediction nor a hollow platitude. It is both our quest and our destiny. *More Disciples* offers us a seasoned and reliable guidebook as we journey to the fulfillment of this great Kingdom venture.

David Garrison
October, 2018
New York, New York

INTRODUCTION

By Curtis Sergeant

Only one life, 'twill soon be past.
Only what's done for Christ will last.
(Refrain from "Only One Life" by C.T. Studd)

In Bethlehem, at the Church of the Nativity, there stands a statue of St. Jerome. He was the translator of the Latin Vulgate, which served as the official Catholic Scriptures from its completion in 416 AD until

the latter half of the 20th century. It is widely considered to be not merely the first translation of the entire Bible, but the most important translation ever.

The Church of the Nativity was built on top of a series of tunnels and caves where Jerome lived and worked on the translation for over 30 years. You will notice when you look at the statue that there is a human skull chained to his left ankle. Jerome lived with that skull chained to his leg in order for it to be a constant reminder to him of the brevity of life. That sort of dedication and focus

Photo 1: Statue of St. Jerome.

1

enabled him to make a massive impact on the world for the Kingdom of God.

In our day, it is perhaps more difficult than ever to maintain such focus. From New Delhi to Beijing, Lagos to São Paulo, London to New York, our increasing urbanization and the integration of new technology into our lives has led to a new sense of busyness and poverty, the poverty of time. Over and over, when seeking to disciple others and equip them to make disciples, I hear objections related to the lack of time.

The last time I checked, everyone still had 24 hours in a day. What has changed?

In Ephesians 2:10, Paul says, "For we are his workmanship, created in Christ Jesus for good works, which God prepared beforehand, that we should walk in them." This tells us that God has specific plans and intentions for what He wants us to do. In the Gospel of John, Jesus repeatedly spoke about the fact that He only said what He heard the Father saying and did only what He saw the Father doing.

My conclusion is that, if we don't have enough time, it must mean that we are not limiting ourselves to what God intends for us to do, but rather we also are seeking to do some activities we want to do. The result is, indeed, we do not have enough time. Similarly, rather than restricting ourselves to saying what the Lord is saying, we spend time saying things we want to say. The result is noise which, when added to the voluminous data our society churns out, fails to achieve the purposes God intends.

It is a matter of stewardship. We must be more in tune with the Spirit in order to utilize the 24 hours we are given each day. We constantly must be attentive to the Lord's intentions and desires in order to achieve His purposes in our communications with others.

Knowing Him and making Him known is the life of being a disciple. Constantly, He is expressing Himself and revealing Himself and communicating to us. He does this in large and bold and loud ways in nature and creation and the rise and fall of empires and the making of history and societal events. He does this in small and intimate and quiet ways through silent impressions and thoughts, dreams, and minute gestures or facial expressions of people. He does it through Scripture, prayer, fellow believers, and pain or grief. To the degree we are sensitive to His communications, we have the opportunity to know Him more intimately and make Him known more effectively.

It is a journey. This journey will not reach its destination until we see Him face to face. We are destined to be "on the way" or "in process" until then. Of course, because He is infinite and we are not, our recognition of Him will always be limited. To the degree we know Him, however, we will be remade more in His image. One purpose of our lives on earth is to begin this process in preparation for an eternity of fellowship with Him and worship of Him forever. The other primary purpose is for Him to use us to be part of His speaking to others.

This book provides tools and concepts to help us develop patterns that support living this sort of life, one that is on a trajectory of knowing Him more fully and making Him known better by others. Some people complain that any tools or patterns are deadening and lifeless and interfere with having a living and vital relationship with God and others. That is ridiculous. We should view such tools and processes in the same way we view eating utensils and mealtimes. Is food boring and bland because we eat with utensils? Does the use of eating utensils ruin the experience of eating? Are meals rendered meaningless because we use a knife, fork, and spoon over and over and over again? Do we lose interest in eating because of the life-draining repetitiveness of the endless cycle of breakfast, lunch, and dinner? Do we quit loving food because of these empty habits?

The tools and concepts in this book provide ways for us to be intentional in listening to God, pursuing the life He intends for us, knowing Him more deeply, making Him known more effectively, and, most importantly, loving Him more passionately. Let us strive to live our lives in an intentional way like St. Jerome in order that we might please the One we love.

In 1 Corinthians 3:10-15 Paul says,

"According to the grace of God given to me, like a skilled master builder I laid a foundation, and someone else is building upon it. Let each one take care how he builds upon it. For no one can lay a foundation other than that which is laid, which is Jesus Christ. Now if anyone builds on the foundation with gold, silver, precious stones, wood, hay, straw - each one's work will become manifest, for the Day will disclose it, because it will be revealed by fire, and the fire will test what sort of work each one has done. If the work that anyone has built on the foundation survives, he will receive a reward. If anyone's work is burned up, he will suffer loss, though he himself will be saved, but only as through fire."

This book provides a toolkit to help us build in this way. May you become a skilled craftsman.

Curtis Sergeant
Dadeville, Alabama
October, 2018

CHAPTER 1

WHY MAKE MORE DISCIPLES

Why should we try to make more disciples? Why should we be in a hurry to do so?

What's a Disciple?

First things first, what do we mean when we say, "disciple?" For the purposes of this book, we'll define a disciple as a follower of Christ who hears, obeys, and shares the Good News with others, then trains them to do the same. Put another way, a disciple loves God, loves people, and makes other disciples. How did we come up with that definition?

Jesus Commanded It

In Matthew's version of the Great Commission, Jesus's command to make disciples of all nations leaves no room for error.

Photo 2: Jesus said, "Make disciples."

Jesus said, "All authority in heaven and on earth has been given to me. Therefore go and make disciples of all nations, baptizing them in the name of the Father and of the Son and of the Holy Spirit, and teaching them to obey everything I have commanded you. And surely I am with you always, to the very end of the age" (Matthew 28:18-20).

If He commanded it, we ought to tackle it full force. There's also another reason why we should want to persuade them.

The Early Church Modeled It

The book of Acts is a history of the expansion of the early Church. The author, Luke, was a very methodical writer. He categorizes himself as a careful investigator (Luke 1:3). He wants his reader(s) to know about the "certainty of things" (Luke 1:4). Although he is aware of multiple secondary sources (Luke 1:1), if he hadn't witnessed something first-hand, he believed in gathering eye-witness reports (Luke 1:2).

Knowing this, it's not surprising that when the first crop of new believers seeks to be baptized into Christ, Luke counts them the best he can. In Acts 2:41, he records that about 3,000 people were added to the number of original disciples following Jesus. I have a feeling this was an estimate, but nevertheless, Luke was trying to investigate properly.

Some six verses later, Luke is already out of fingers. By this time (already), God was adding to their numbers daily those who were being saved (Acts 2:47).

Interestingly, as persecution broke out, it didn't stifle Kingdom growth. It just amplified it. When Peter and John were imprisoned because they couldn't stop testifying about the resurrected Jesus, it prompted some 5,000 new believers to accept Christ (Acts 4:3). By the time we get to Acts 5:32, the believers were meeting needs of the poor like crazy, as a natural outgrowth of their love and concern for one another. God did some amazing things during those days (Acts 5:12). A few verses (and a few days) later, Luke has to admit, he can't keep track any more. At that point, instead of guessing at the numbers, he just quantifies them as "increasing numbers — crowds of both men and women" (Acts 5:14). This reminds me of a child who, instead of counting, will just give up and begin to use words like "gobs" and "humongous" and "mongo."

More persecution breaks out. More punishment takes place. The growth skyrockets. The disciples are meeting daily —not just in the temple complex, but in homes too (Acts 5:42). Every day, they keep "teaching and proclaiming the good news that Jesus is the Messiah" (also in Acts 5:42). The government and religious leaders ratchet up the persecution even more and what happens to the church? "So the preaching about God flourished, the number of the disciples in Jerusalem multiplied greatly, and a large group of priests became obedient to the faith" (Acts 6:7).

Luke was astounded. From his roots as a critical investigative reporter, he saw growth out of control. In fact, the early Church went from exact numbers to additions, then from additions to additions **daily**, and from daily additions to **multiplication**.

Now **that** is what we call **more disciples**.

Love Compels Us

If we truly believe in a literal place of eternal punishment for those who don't know Jesus (2 Thess. 1:8-9), then it stands to reason that loving Christians would do everything they can to get the message out as quickly as possible to save as many as possible. You see, researchers tell us that approximately 2.9 billion people in the world today are unreached by circumstance, not by choice. They've never had a valid chance to say "Yes!" to Jesus because they don't have a significant witness in their midst. How much would we have to **hate** them to keep the truth a secret — especially when we know how to retell it?

To make matters even more complicated, these 2.9 billion people don't all speak the same language. In fact, many wouldn't even speak to one another if they did! They are separated by barriers of geography, culture, understanding, and/or acceptance. Since their fathers and forefathers wouldn't speak to one another, their descendants follow in those same footsteps. They might shop in the same market. Maybe they even attend the same university; however, because of language, resentment, ethnicity, or simple pride, they don't hang together. So reaching one population segment is no guarantee of reaching the neighboring group.

When we begin to count all those differing tribes, languages, castes, and nations, the numbers swell quickly. Many of these groups will need unique strategies because they are unique "people groups." The old song, "Each one, reach one," breaks down when the "one" won't talk to the other. Nope, to reach all people groups, the effort is going to have to be intentional.

Our Complex World Demands a Solution

Add to this the challenge of today's cities. Over half the people in the world today live in urban areas. Take London, for instance. In a 2015 study, 33% of all Londoners said they believe in an afterlife, but 41% reported that they believed we simply "cease to exist" after death, and another 26% weren't sure. Today roughly 1/3 of all adults in Britain claim they don't believe in "a God." So megacities which were once missionary-sending centers are now confused about and even negative about Christianity (Jordan, 2015).

If this is true, then today's church faces a virtual emergency. Every day, among all these tribes, castes, and nations, some 50,000 to 70,000 people pass into a Christless eternity with no hope of Heaven. Unless God "changes His mind" about judgment, the certainty is — they will not enjoy His Heaven.

Caring for the One

In Luke 15, Jesus tells the story of the shepherd who left 99 sheep in a meadow in the high country and combed the hillsides, picking His way in and out of ledges and briar patches, in hopes of finding one lost lamb. How much the more, with 2.9 BILLION lost souls, should we make it a priority to "leave the 99" in the high country and mobilize every last resource available for the sake of the **last,** the **least,** and the **lost**—the most **desperate** living in the greatest **darkness** in the most imminent **danger.**

In Steven Spielberg's 1993 blockbuster movie, *Schindler's List*, based on an actual man's life, Liam Neeson's character, Oskar Schindler, arrives in Krakow in 1939, hoping to make a good living running his new factory. He joins with the Nazis at first because it was smart for business.

He fills his factory with Jewish workers for smart-business reasons. And when Hitler's troops begin wiping out nearby Jewish settlements, Schindler protects his workers, perhaps in the beginning, mainly to keep his factory running smoothly. Soon, he becomes passionate about saving innocent lives. In a famous scene, with the help of his Jewish accountant, played by Ben Kingsley, he works hard to develop a list in which every life mattered. He can be heard to say again and again, "How many are on the list now?" Again at the end of the movie, he's asking, "Why didn't I sell my car? Why didn't I sell this pen?" Of course Schindler is moved by the gratitude of the 1,200 he has saved, but he's filled with anguish that he didn't save "just one more."

Photo 3: Jesus said, "Go after the lost sheep."

Add to God's Glory

There's another reason for making more disciples that goes beyond the imminent justice of God. And that is, the glory of God. John Piper wrote,

"Missions is not the ultimate goal of the church. Worship is. Missions exists because worship doesn't. Worship is ultimate, not missions, because God is ultimate, not man. When this age is over, and the countless millions of the redeemed fall on their faces before the throne of God, missions will be no more. It is a temporary necessity. But worship abides forever. So worship is the fuel and goal of missions" (Piper, 2010).

Making more disciples means more people wearing white robes (headed to Heaven) at the end of all time. No one should go to his grave without someone testifying to him about Christ's love. And more disciples add to God's glory, by adding to the praises that will be uttered by a tapestry of skin-tones, cultures, and races.

If we could possibly accelerate the fulfillment of the Great Commission, should not every church, every household, and every individual in God's Kingdom want to get involved? What if these approaches helped us save millions, or thousands, or even just one more lost lamb? Should it not become our highest priority?

There's No Time to Waste

In view of all the above, there's no time to waste. If we could discover an approach that might accelerate good Kingdom growth, should we not embrace it? Curtis Sergeant's (who wrote the foreword for this book) famous 12-minute training video shows the importance of the speed at which we tell the Good News to the unreached. When he begins telling about pace, he begins snapping his fingers loudly, explaining that, with each snap, another soul is passing into a Christ-less eternity. About 50,000 people per day die among all unreached peoples — which roughly corresponds to one person every second (Sergeant, YouTube, 2015). In view of the millions (billions, actually) with little or no message, shouldn't today's highest priority be "more disciples" and "more training" in an effort to reach as many as possible, among as many neighbors and nations as possible?

Curtis reiterated a call to action in a recent article he wrote for *Mission Frontiers*.

It would be simple to think someone else will step up and answer the call. It would be tragic if we sat hopeless in a broken world when we are the ones He put here to co-labor with Him to do something about it.

In America: Only 2% of Christians share their faith. Let's do something about it – in Jesus's name!

In the last 10 years, church attendance has gone down in every single county. Let's do something about it – in Jesus's name!

In the last 10 years, church membership dropped nearly 10% and population increased 11.4%. Let's do something about it – in Jesus's name!

Transfer growth and the conversion of children of existing members account for 96% of church growth. Let's do something about it – in Jesus's name!

Of all Americans, 53% are now considered "uninvitable to church." Let's do something about it – in Jesus's name!

Our cities and states are becoming increasingly unreached. Let's do something about it – in Jesus's name!

Other religions like Islam, Hinduism, Atheism, and Secularism are shaping society. Let's do something about it – in Jesus's name!

We all have seen or heard of movements taking place in China, India, Africa, and many other places by the hand of the Lord. Now, it is America's time. Let us believe this in faith!

As God rhetorically asked in His first book, "Is anything too hard for the Lord" (Sergeant, The Zume Project Igniting The Spark, 2018)?

In Matthew 9:35-36, we read about Jesus's heart for the hurting. Matthew records that "when Jesus saw the crowds, he had compassion on them." Why did he have compassion? Because "they were harassed and helpless, like sheep without a shepherd." Have you ever seen crowds like that? Have you met the harassed and helpless? Do some of them live next door? If that's the case, imagine what it's like in a refugee camp in Europe, or a remote village in Africa, or in a crowded village with dirt streets beside a river in Asia. In Matthew 9:37, Jesus concluded, "The harvest is plentiful but the workers are few. Ask the Lord of the harvest, therefore, to send out workers into his harvest field." Today, will you join me in that prayer for the harvest?

Questions for Discussion:

1. How might you have previously answered the question, "What is a disciple?" Do you agree or disagree with the definition provided in this chapter?

2. How did you view disciple-making before reading this chapter? Compare and contrast your prior understanding with any nuances you've picked up from this reading.

3. This chapter pointed to the fact that the early church seemed all the more to thrive in the midst of persecution. Would you say there is persecution where you will be making disciples? Has the church thrived? Offer some theories as to why or why not?

4. How might you have previously explained the parable of the lost sheep in Luke 15? As a result of reading this chapter, how has your understanding changed, if at all?

5. If a friend were to ask, "Does making more disciples somehow add to the global voice offering glory to God," how would you answer? Explain the basis of your position.

CHAPTER 2

A WAY FORWARD

If we accept the premise that God wants us to make more disciples, the question then arises, "How?" Accepting that God desires and expects us to join Him in this task, how do we go forward?

Researchers and practitioners have sought an answer to that very question for 100 years or so. Today, we stand on the shoulders of giants who have enlightened the way through years of exploration and experimentation, seeking the answer to the key question in this book: "How can we make more disciples?"

Photo 4: To make more disciples, what's the "way forward?"

Today, we are in the midst of what just might be the greatest awakening since the first century. We are witnessing, in fact, what can only be described as a vast sea change in the way we believe God wants us to participate in growing His kingdom. This paradigm shift is huge. As we look back at the past 100 years, suddenly, in what seems like the blink of an eye, the earth has shifted.

Allen

It's hard to find the absolute beginning of this journey, so let's just pick one modern-day prophet and let him represent the awakening many others have been experiencing. Roland Allen is one of the best expressions for our wake-up call today. In *The Spontaneous Expansion of the Church* (Allen, 1962), written in 1927, Allen imagined a day when **every** believer would tell the gospel story to everyone he or she met. This constant proclamation, coupled with the work of the Holy Spirit, would, in Allen's opinion, unleash a power in the church known only before in the book of Acts. The church would grow like wildfire. All believers, when freed of outside controlling factors, would instinctively long to spread a burning faith because they simply couldn't keep quiet.

Patterson

Fast-forward a few decades and you'll hear another prophet, a little-known missionary named George Patterson. In his book, *Obedience-Oriented Education* (Patterson, 1976), Patterson compared traditional college methods with what he called, "obedience-oriented methods." He wrote, "The obedience-oriented teacher, looking beyond his student, is satisfied only with edifying work in the field" (Patterson, 1976, p. 3). Patterson saw a day when the church would grow spontaneously.

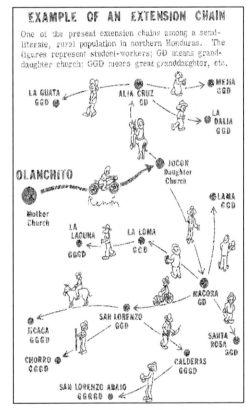

EXAMPLE OF AN EXTENSION CHAIN

One of the present extension chains among a semi-literate, rural population in northern Honduras. The figures represent student-workers; GD means granddaughter church; GGD means great granddaughter, etc.

Figure 5: Patterson's vision of small extension classes look a lot like the multiplying groups of CPM/DMM.

Like all living creatures, the Church has within herself the power to grow and multiply after her own kind (Mark 4:1-20). She develops spontaneously, not like an institution whose progress depends on the initiative of her executives. An active, feeling body, she seethes with potential energy. An obedient church has to grow and multiply just as surely as the plants and animals; it is her nature. This assurance moves us to witness and serve in relaxed, voluntary obedience to Christ (Patterson, 1976, p. 15-16).

Patterson describes (and pictures) an Extension Chain. This Extension Chain diagram clearly shows that a worker (I wrote in the name, Ramon) from a "mother church" (in Olanchito) would end up riding a motorcycle to a nearby town called Jocon, where he would begin spreading the Good News and raising up a church. From there, two other workers would end up traveling to towns like Alta Cruz and Macora. There, these two workers would establish what Patterson called "granddaughter churches." Workers would leave towns like Alta Cruz to travel to other villages like La Guata, Mejia, and La Dalia, where these new workers would establish "great granddaughter" churches. Patterson concluded from his personal observations that the churches with little or no contact with professional missionaries were actually the strongest and most trouble-free. However, he pointed out that there was a constant channel of communication going up and down the chain. He loved it that "everyone in the chain knows what is going on in his own area of responsibility" (Patterson, 1976, p. 18).

Patterson developed a terrific work in Honduras, modeled after the early Church in the book of Acts. Just as Luke had trouble tracking all the multiplication, Patterson had some trouble, too. Patterson writes later,

> "To permit a spontaneous movement in the churches the theological curriculum itself forms part of the multiplying process. The students become teachers of others; their assignments aim to develop new leaders in an atmosphere of freedom to work for Christ" (Patterson, 1976, p. 12).

By keeping the churches (or classes) rather small, the student-workers could achieve success rather rapidly.

Patterson characterized this process as "Small Extension Classes," explaining that "Reteaching the same things to their own congregations or classes readily reproduces new centers of leadership" (Patterson, 1976, p. 28).

Patterson said, "Traditional textbooks do not lend themselves to a spontaneous movement. To adapt to a program of self-extension, each textbook should (1) be self-teaching, (2) require corresponding practical work for each week's study, and (3) be reteachable, enabling any student-worker to reteach it to his own students in another center" (p. 29). He later adds, "Tradition cripples spontaneous expansion by limiting evangelism to special meetings or Sunday evening services. Biblically, evangelism is the ordinary, daily work of the members of a church. There is nothing special about it. But some churches leave witnessing for professionals with extraordinary preparation" (Patterson, 1976, p. 30).

I love it that Patterson was so practical. He developed a list of 35 activities in which each student-worker needed to engage. "Student-workers

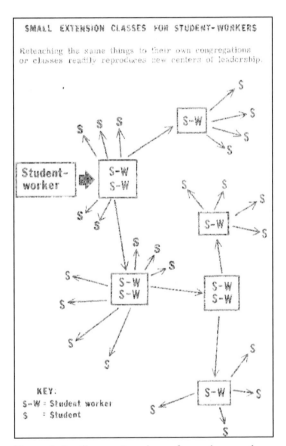

Figure 6: Small extension classes for student-workers.

16

do almost all their own theoretical studies during their own time." He expanded, "There are no long-term courses in Bible, history or doctrine" (Patterson, 1976, p. 33). Instead of telling each worker what to believe, he taught the student-workers how to revere the Bible as the highest authority. The student-workers learned on the job — and Patterson's model grew, not unlike the book of Acts. God helped him grow from one family to 100 churches in just 15 years (Lucas, 2017). The guy is like an Energizer Bunny. He just won't quit. When I tracked him down to see if we could interview him for a webinar, I finally found him in an assisted-living home in Florida. He chuckled that I remembered his little booklet. What was he doing that week? Writing a series of training materials for a church in Cincinnati, Ohio, which wanted to strengthen its ability to multiply members and groups. (Lord, please raise up more workers like George Patterson.)

McGavran

Donald McGavran, a contemporary to Patterson, was the son of missionary parents in India. While growing up, he noticed that sometimes whole villages and entire districts would come to Christ in what he called "multi-individual, mutually-interdependent people movements." He first described these phenomena in a little book called *Bridges of God* (McGavran D. , 1975) in 1955, then refined and improved his ideas in *Understanding Church Growth* (McGavran D. , 1976). McGavran was a bit of a scientist. He introduced, or at least made popular, the concept of applying survey and research methodology toward church growth. This unlocked a new science, allowing us to measure what works, opening up a new doorway of understanding the way God's Kingdom expands.

Garrison

The table was set. Building on McGavran's case study methodology, David Garrison next wrote what could only be described as a landmark work, *Church Planting Movements* (Garrison, Church Planting Movements, 2004). Garrison had been hearing of isolated cases in which many people, sometimes hundreds of thousands of nonbelievers, were coming in droves embracing faith in Christ, and immediately sharing their testimonies, often in the face of severe persecution. Garrison referred to these experiences as **church-planting movements, defining them as "a rapid multiplication of indigenous churches planting churches that sweeps through a people group or population segment"** (Garrison, Church Planting Movements, 2004, p. 7).

In dozens of movements around the world, he began to see recurring themes. After some time, he concluded that there were at least 10 of these recurring patterns, so common that he referred to them as "universal elements" (Garrison, Church Planting Movements, 2004, pp. 33-36):

1. **Prayer**: Prayer was fundamental to every church planting movement. Garrison determined that when the initial disciple-maker had a strong vitality of prayer, personally, new believers seemed to pick it up and imitate it naturally.

2. **Abundant gospel sowing**: Garrison noted that the law of the harvest reigned in all the movements he studied, meaning, "If you sow abundantly you will also reap abundantly." Each of the movements he studied had multiplied with the help of what could only be described as insane amounts of evangelism.

3. **Intentional church planting**: Garrison saw many evangelistic awakenings. For those awakenings to become church planting movements, he noted that someone in the mix (usually a missionary from the outside) had implanted the concept of deliberate church multiplication as the goal.

4. **Scriptural authority**: In every instance, Scripture provided the rudder for the new movement's life, and its authority was unquestioned. This made possible rapid multiplication - because everyone was multiplying the very same message, as inspired directly by the Word of God.

5. **Local leadership:** Garrison noted that, in each case, these movements were occurring when the outsider (the missionary) took on the role of a mentor or coach rather than directly pastoring the people involved.

6. **Lay leadership:** In the case studies he documented, growth had become exponential only when leaders were typically bivocational, meaning that they made their living through a job other than serving as clergy. What's more, leaders typically came from the same general profile as the profile of the vast majority of the people themselves. He noted that paid clergy often emerged as the movement unfolded, but he saw that the majority (the growing edge) of the movement centered in lay leaders. He concluded that depending on seminary-trained leaders always resulted in a leadership deficit in rapidly-growing movements.

7. **Cell or house churches:** Garrison saw a trend — the vast majority of churches in these movements tended to be small (10-30) and they most often met in homes or storefronts rather than in buildings purchased for meeting places. In the movements he studied, Garrison saw both cell churches (organized meetings arranged by the leadership core of the movement) and house churches (more dynamic in nature and not necessarily arranged by a central leadership core).

8. **Churches planting churches:** In the cases Garrison analyzed, he noted that no matter what **started** things, by the time the growth became multiplicative (a true movement), it was multiplying into other churches along a chain of growth that contained a kind of electricity that was dynamic. It existed in order to grow.

9. **Rapid reproduction:** Every single movement Garrison studied, had become rampant growth. Rapid reproduction essentially fueled the growing edge of the movement. For this to take place, Garrison noted that churches needed to be free of extra encum-

brances (nonessential elements) such as buildings, programs, budgets, and perhaps even paid staff.

10. **Healthy churches**: It goes without saying that movements only occurred when the churches within them were largely healthy. In other words, they focused on 1) worship, 2) evangelism and missionary outreach, 3) education and discipleship, 4) ministry and 5) fellowship. In each of the cases he found, these five core functions were evident. In fact, he noticed that when these five health indicators were strong, churches couldn't help but grow.

Garrison felt so strongly about the above threads that he called them "universals," necessary for every church-planting initiative. He also observed other characteristics, which he called "common elements," that were **often**, though not universally present. These are helpful because they describe **many** movements, even if not every case (Garrison, Church Planting Movements, 2004, pp. 37-40):

1. **Worship in the heart language:** Garrison observed that when missionaries chose to work through a trade language, it seemed to create a virtual curtain between themselves and the hearts of the people they were seeking to reach.

2. **Evangelism has communal implications:** More often than not, movements had grown along family or social connections. Churches, then, were essentially like extended families, with the family head serving as the church leader. (Garrison has theorized that this is one of the reasons these types of movements aren't seen as often in the

Photo 7: Evangelism has communal implications.

West, where individualism and personal commitment are the predominant pattern.)

3. **Rapid incorporation of new converts into the life and ministry of the church:** Interestingly, Garrison observed that in most church planting movements, baptism was not delayed by lengthy discipleship requirements. On the contrary, discipleship typically preceded conversion and continued indefinitely. Newly-baptized believers were expected immediately to begin leading others to Christ.

4. **Passion and fearlessness:** After studying dozens of these movements, Garrison concluded that boldness may invite persecution, but it fuels church planting. In fact, he also concluded that the corollary was true as well. A spirit of timidity or fear quenches a church-planting movement.

5. **A price to pay to become a Christian:** Surprisingly, in Garrison's study, church planting movements often emerged in difficult settings where conversion to the gospel of Jesus Christ was not socially an advantageous thing to do. In many cases, conversion led to severe persecution or even death. Persecution acted as a kind of filter, screening out all but the most dedicated members. Those same members became the backbone of a dependable movement.

6. **Perceived leadership crisis or spiritual vacuum in society:** Again, though it might not seem intuitive, when society became unstable, movements grew all the more. The void created by loss of dependable social structures apparently demanded that members find stability in something other than political realms.

7. **On-the-job training for church leadership:** Fast-growing movements do not allow the luxury of time to send prospective leaders off for academic degrees. Training had to be refined into something that could be done "on the job," and, therefore, leadership for the movement became intrinsically more reproducible.

8. **Leadership authority decentralized**: Garrison's studies involved movements too dynamic to be led by controlling authorities. In fact, Garrison concluded that movements grew best when the leaders of each house or cell church could act interdependently, without having to seek permission from a higher authority.

9. **Low profile of outsiders**: In the movements that Garrison studied, rather than waiting for new believers to prove themselves worthy of leadership, missionaries drew new believers into leadership roles through participative Bible studies and mentoring them into the role of pastor from behind the scenes.

10. **Suffering of missionaries**: Interestingly, Garrison saw another trend. Many of those who started things experienced derision and shame; many even encountered illness and suffering. Garrison wondered if this might be due to direct attacks by Satan. Garrison noted Revelation 12:12, "Therefore rejoice, you heavens and you who dwell in them! But woe to the earth and the sea, because the devil has gone down to you! He is filled with fury, because he knows that his time is short" (Garrison, Church Planting Movements, 2004, p. 40).

This might be as good of a time as any to deal with the five terms (acronyms) being used to refer to this growth by movements.

- **CPM:** Church-planting movement
- **CMM:** Church multiplication movement
- **SCMM:** Sustainable church multiplication movement
- **T4T:** Training for trainers
- **DMM:** Disciple-making movement

Regardless of the exact term used, these terms all tend to describe a situation in which a disciple-maker (like Paul) shares his faith with a new disciple (like Timothy), then immediately begins training Timothy to share his faith with another individual. Timothy then trains this new disciple, in turn, to share his testimony with another, and so on.

If it's beginning to sound a lot like 2 Timothy 2:2, then you're getting it: "And the things you have heard me say in the presence of many witnesses entrust to reliable people who will also be qualified to teach others."

Analyzing this verse, one might think of a family tree, of sorts, like Patterson's "extension chain." Each new link is like a new spiritual generation, and when these generations happen in fairly rapid succession, the whole thing can go viral, resulting in amazing rapid growth. What we're describing is nothing short of Roland Allen's "spontaneous expansion of the church," rapid-fire. It's Patterson, except, instead of 15 years, it's crunched down to 18 months. And just as nuclear scientists try to reach critical mass in a nuclear energy plant, church multiplication trainers are constantly searching for the secret sauce to reach the tipping point in fostering a church multiplication movement.

How exactly do we FOSTER that movement? What are the catalysts that accelerate the chain reaction?

Well — that's the subject of the rest of this book. In some ways, it's all very simple. (It's all written up in the book of Acts.) Yes, there are indeed several practices and personal spiritual habits involved. And as we've said before, all of this is dependent on the work of the Holy Spirit in our midst. There are no magic wands, no guarantees, and no easy "drive-through" short-cuts. It seems that we can work as hard as we want — but only GOD brings about a true movement. Movements are, in many ways, one of His mod-ern-day miracles.

Photo 8: Movements depend on the work of the Spirit.

24:14

Our final voice isn't just one person, but is, in fact, a coalition which is using the name, "24:14," after the biblical passage, Matthew 24:14, in which Jesus says, "This good news of the kingdom will be proclaimed in all the world as a testimony to all nations. And then the end will come."

The 24:14 consortium publishes a monthly update (24:14, 2018). In their July, 2018 update, they defined and further described a church-planting movement (CPM) or disciple-making movement (DMM).

In the 24:14 coalition, we view a Church Planting Movement (CPM)/ Disciple Making Movement (DMM) approach as one in which:

1. There is awareness that only God can start movements. As disciples we can, however, follow biblical principles to pray, plant, and water the seeds that can lead to movements like those we see in Acts.

2. The focus is to make every follower of Christ a reproducing disciple rather than merely a convert.

3. Simple patterns are used which create frequent and regular accountability for both obeying what the Lord is speaking to each person and for him to pass it on to others in a loving environment. This requires a participative small-group approach.

4. Each disciple is equipped in comprehensive ways (such as interpreting and applying Scripture, a well-rounded prayer life, functioning as a part of the larger Body of Christ, and responding well to persecution/suffering) in order that he might function not merely as a consumer, but as an active agent of Kingdom advance.

5. Each disciple is given a vision both for reaching his relational network and for extending the Kingdom to the ends of the earth with a prioritization on the darkest places (with a "no place left" mentality - Rom. 15:23). They are equipped to be able to minister and partner with others in the Body of Christ in both of these environments.

6. Reproducing churches are intentionally formed as a part of the process of multiplying disciples. The intent in CPM/DMM approaches is that 1) disciples, 2) churches, 3) leaders and 4) movements can multiply endlessly by the power of the Spirit.
7. Emphasis is not on the specific model of CPM/DMM used, but on the underlying biblical principles of multiplying kingdom movements.

They added and clarified, "24:14 often uses 'CPM' as an all-encompassing term to refer to movements, but endorses both CPM and DMM as legitimate terms to describe the same process and believes there are many movement approaches and variations that work effectively depending on the cultural context."

So, let's summarize the descriptions being used by 24:14 in defining these Kingdom movements:

1. Spirit-led
2. Every follower a multiplier
3. Peer accountability
4. Become a disciple worth multiplying
5. Here, near, and far-vision
6. Multiplying disciples, churches, leaders, and movements
7. Emphasizing **biblical** principles of multiplication

Summary: A Call for Action

Having established the need for making more disciples in chapter 1, we can now see a clear path forward (this chapter). In the rest of this book, then, we will deliver practical "lessons learned" about how to become a catalyst for these Kingdom movements. We hope this manual can be a step-by-step guidebook, a template, of sorts. We hope that, using this book, you, the reader, can implement the fruitful "best practices" being used across the globe today in real-time.

CPM/DMM trainers emphasize that for too long churches have emphasized content and knowledge over action and obedience. We have talked about "being present in church every time the doors are open," as if membership in the club is equivalent to making disciples. It's not.

Making disciples requires action. Even the Great Commission itself assumed that we would be "going." Actually, in the original language, "go" is a present participle that some translators would translate, "as you are going," perhaps alluding to the fact that Jesus just assumed they would be excited about sharing the Good News.

The strong force of the verse rests in the phrase, "make disciples," in the imperative or command mode. **"As you are going, make disciples."** This shift in thinking to a command for action requires, we believe, a fundamental paradigm shift for many (most?) local church members.

Robert M. Reach, in his book, *Movements that Move* (Reach, 2016), writes,

In Western understanding, based on Greek worldview, we tend to think that if someone understands a concept then they own it. Comprehension is everything. If I can repeat the information, then it is mine. The Western model of learning focuses on information absorption, which is typically done in a classroom with an instructor and minimal participation by the learner. Of course there are exceptions to this practice, and my hope is that you've participated in one of those exceptions whether in an educational institution or a church. However, there is significant contrast with what happens in movements that move (p. 73).

As Patterson put it, it's a "relaxed, voluntary obedience to Christ," not a series of binding "works" that we have to do to be saved. Obedience arises from gratitude for His mercy, then wells up as a result of being "compelled by His love" (2 Corinthians 5:14). We are therefore convinced that we simply HAVE to serve as His ambassadors (2 Cor. 5:20), not out of a heavy burden of obligation or guilt, but rather because He has already reconciled us to Himself (2 Cor. 5:18). We serve because He has already made us into new creations and all our "old things" have passed away (2 Cor. 5:17). May God be praised!

So, one of the core exhortations in this book is the need for a major shift: from being mere hearers (of sermons on Sunday morning or of Christian music in our cars) to doers who multiply in our own version of Patterson's "extension chain." This book is **a call for action**.

It will be tempting to read about these strategies, practices, and habits and then to say, "OK, I've got this," and not do anything. But at its core, implementing these life practices and strategies isn't about "knowing something." It's about living the Bible among those who don't. It's about following a set of principles and practices that, when implemented and blessed by the Spirit of God, foster a reprisal of the book of Acts all over again in our day-to-day lives. And we're suggesting that, if possible, all of us who have accepted Christ should be content with no less.

Thus, please, don't sit back. Lean into this book and let's set our sails for the voyage ahead.

Photo 9: Let's set our sails for the voyage ahead.

Questions for Discussion:

1. Roland Allen's books weren't published until some 50 years after he wrote them. Why do you suppose it took a while for others to see value in his writings? (Try doing some research online about this question.)

2. Some have ventured that Patterson's approach was remarkably similar to CPM/DMM approaches used today -- and it was plainly very effective for his time. Yet it can be said that relatively few churches/workers implemented his strategies. Why do you think it's seemingly difficult for churches and leaders to change the way they do disciple-making? How might we shift the future?

3. McGavran witnessed whole villages and sometimes entire districts coming to Christ at once. Try to picture being involved in something like that. How would it change the way you felt about evangelism and church growth? Explain.

4. Pick one of Garrison's universal elements that you believe is commonly misunderstood or about which people today have a misconception. Offer some ideas as to why.

5. Garrison is a researcher. He found that the 10 Universal Elements were present in every movement toward Christ that he studied. How many of these elements might exist in the church that you attend or in the field where you hope to make disciples? How might you be a part of changing the future there?

CHAPTER 3

DISCIPLE-MAKING WORKS

Movements Make the Difference

David Garrison studied CPM/DMM all around the world. Most of the reports in these paragraphs come from both the first chapter of his book, *Church-Planting Movements*, and stories he has told during live trainings for our organization, Team Expansion.

Garrison tells of a worker in Ethiopia who had managed to start four churches in 30 years in the field. Then, with a slight change in their approach, 65 churches were formed in just nine months. In a field in Latin America, one stream of churches went from an active membership of 5,800 up to 14,000 in one decade and was running 38,000 at last count. In another nearby region, a group went from 129 congregations to 1,918 in just ten years. Membership went from 7,000 to nearly 16,000. Another movement in Asia went from 85 believers in 1991 to 55,000 believers in 1998, the number of churches from a handful to more than 550. In India, a stream of churches went from 28 congregations to 2000. In seven years, 55,000 local people came to Christ. And, among the Khmer of Cambodia one stream of churches grew from 600 to more than 60,000.

Garrison also shares of God's amazing work in Southeast Asia which started with three churches and 85 believers among a population of 7 million. Four years later, God had established a movement with more than 550 churches and nearly 55,000 believers. Garrison documented another work in North Africa where an Arab Muslim cleric complained that more than 10,000 Muslims in the surrounding mountains had apostatized from Islam and become Christians. And in a city in China, Garrison found that over a four-year period (1993-1997), more than 20,000 people had come to faith in Christ, resulting in over 500 new churches. In Latin America, a movement grew from 235 churches in 1990 to more than 3,200 in 1998. And in an area in Central Asia, believers grew from 200 to 15,000 in just one year. Garrison continues to track these movements — 30,000 believers in a Southeast Asian country, 100,000 believers growing by 800 new churches in eastern India, 20,000 conversions in just four years in a region of China, church launches doubling inside of six months in a Western European country, and 383 churches starting in just one state in Brazil.

In *A Wind in the House of Islam* (Garrison, A Wind in the House of Islam, 2014), Garrison chronicled a movement among Shi'ite Muslims in Iran in the 1980's (Garrison, A Wind in the House of Islam, 2014, p. 16), a movement among Kabyle Berbers in Algeria that resulted in thousands coming to Christ throughout North Africa, and in the 1990s a movement among Turkic Central Asian groups. He describes 1000 new Disciples in Albania and Bulgaria. And he tells the story of tens of thousands of Bengali Muslims seeking out baptism and faith in Jesus at the turn of the century. In fact, in the final two decades of the 20th century, he chronicles no fewer than 13 movements away from Muslim communities toward Christ.

We're seeing the beginnings of a CPM/DMM in our own organization, Team Expansion, in a Muslim field in West Africa. The workers there had worked for nearly a decade and won around 30 to Christ. We actually thought they were doing okay since most of the people they were seeking to reach were Muslim and work is slow among Muslims. However, after a training in July 2010 on disciple-making movements, the workers went back and began implementing the strategies. It made an immediate difference. In one year alone (2017) they, together with the nationals they were training, started 380 groups and had a total of

529 groups meeting. That same year they baptized 1650 people and had 3,434 people attending Bible study groups. And there's no end in sight. During 2018, the movement baptized 3,511 people and started 794 new simple church groups. This is the power of the Holy Spirit working mightily through CPM/DMM approaches.

Jerry Trousdale has written in *The Kingdom Unleashed* that though Christianity is spreading faster now than it has at any time in human history, it is mainly holding its own in the Global North while exploding in the Global South. (When we use the term, "Global North," we are typically describing countries that are economically more developed. In short, they are richer. These would be countries like the United States, Canada, Europe, Japan, Macau, Brunei, and Israel as well as Australia and New Zealand. When we say, "Global South," we are describing much of the rest of the world, including lands like Africa, Latin America, and developing Asia, including the Middle East.) Consider the following from *Kingdom Unleashed* (Trousdale, 2018, pp. 31-32):

- There were nine million Christians in Africa in 1900; by 2000, there were 335 million (37 times as many) with most of the growth occurring since the 1960s.
- In Latin America in 1900, there were 50,000 Protestants; today, there are more than 64 million (1,280 times as many), again with most of the growth occurring since the 1960s.
- The number of Christians in Asia grew from 101 million to 351 million between 1970 and 2010.
- In China, it has been estimated that 10,000 people per day become disciples. Even by conservative estimates, Christianity there has grown 4,300 percent in 50 years.
- There are now 3.7 times as many Protestants in Africa as in North America – and the gap grows dramatically every year.
- In 1980, sixty-five percent of the world's missionaries were sent out from the Global North; by 2020, that situation will be reversed, as sixty-three percent will be coming from the Global South.

We're convinced that multiplication like this can happen in the Global North someday, too. Unfortunately, the sails of the Global North seem to be catching the wind a bit more slowly than much of the rest of the world.

Case Studies Too Sensitive to Write

There are literally hundreds of stories NOT yet written in books. I recently interviewed a worker in Asia who has watched God bring about a church-planting movement that now has grown to include over 20,000 believers. Literally **all** the group leadership is being provided by local people. The really wild thing is that this movement is just one of THREE such movements on the same set of islands in Asia.

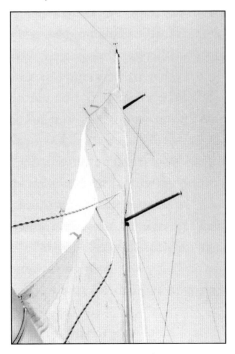

Photo 10: The sails of the Global North seem to be catching the wind a bit more slowly.

It's like God has chosen this vehicle (CPM/DMM) to visit and empower His people in this era. God is truly at work.

Can Movements Like These Happen in North America?

We're convinced that the answer to this question has to be an emphatic yes. However, Trousdale has written that there are only eight or so movements being tracked in all of North America, Western Europe, and Oceania combined (Trousdale, 2018, p. 34). We have seen the beginnings of promising growth in cities like Indianapolis, Kansas City, West Palm Beach and Louisville. And the movement in Tampa, Florida, gives us even more hope. There, God has worked through a former drug addict to raise up the beginnings of a movement consisting of hundreds of groups and thousands of Disciples. (Learn more about Lee Wood's story on the More Disciples podcast, http://www.moredisciples.com/webinars.)

What could help the Global North catch on to CPM/DMM strategies and life principles all the more? One proposal is a new course called Zúme, a web-driven training experience with 10 sessions focused on becoming a disciple worth multiplying. It also teaches personal and group-oriented CPM/DMM strategies to share our faith and grow the church. (ZumeProject, 2018). (We'll talk a lot more about Zúme later.)

A pastor named Ron recently tried Zúme. He wrote the following testimony:

> Several months ago a friend asked me to look at the Zúme Project website. ... What I discovered there was... a simple, easily transferable way of multiplying disciples led by and sustained by ordinary people. [Now, months later,...] Zúme has ignited something in the Mid-Atlantic. Kingdom fruit is being harvested by people who have never allowed God to use them to reach their friends and neighbors. People are prayer walking their neighborhoods and engaging in gospel conversations. And best of all, this is happening without it becoming just another program that flames up but soon burns out. People "want" to do Zúme rather than having to be pushed or guilted into making disciples. I wish I would have had these tools 30 years ago, but thank God that He placed them in my hands at 60! This truly is a Mid-Atlantic movement that is actually moving!

Let's pray that Zúme can help push the Global North forward in its implementation of CPM/DMM principles and life practices.

Questions for Discussion:

1. Describe the growth you've seen so far in the church you attend or in the field where you hope to make disciples. Compare or

contrast this with the case studies illustrated in this chapter. Why might God bring about such movements in one part of the world but not in another? Explain as best you can.

2. Some of these stories seem almost beyond belief. Yet researchers like Garrison have actually visited and verified the fruit. Imagine how you might feel as you interview members of the 27th generation of disciples in a rapidly-growing movement toward Christ. How would that impact your faith in or walk with Christ? Explain.

3. Does it bother you that the Global South might end up sending more missionaries than historically mission-active regions like the USA, Europe and Australia? Why or why not?

4. Does it bother you that the church is growing faster in the Global South than in the Global North? Offer some of your own theories as to why this might be taking place.

5. Do you believe movements like these can happen in North America? Why or why not?

CHAPTER 4

PRAYER IS THE CATALYST

Everywhere we turn, we hear trainers emphasizing the importance of prayer as the fundamental catalyst to launch a movement.

Jesus taught His disciples in Matthew 9:35-38 to "ask the Lord of the harvest" to raise up harvesters. We must learn to ask the Lord for that miracle. At the end of the day, multiplying disciples and groups is a spiritual battle, not a tactical one. So it should come as no surprise that all of the instructions for spiritual battle apply fully.

> Put on the full armor of God, so that you can take your stand against the devil's schemes. For our struggle is not against flesh and blood, but against the rulers, against the authorities, against the powers of this dark world and against the spiritual forces of evil in the heavenly realms. Therefore put on the full armor of God, so that when the day of evil comes, you may be able to stand your ground. . . . And pray in the Spirit on all occasions with all kinds of prayers and requests. With this in mind, be alert and always keep on praying for all the Lord's people . . . [and] me . . . an ambassador in chains. Pray that I may declare [the gospel] fearlessly, as I should (Ephesians 6:10-20).

In 2010, prior to attending a training in the Philippines on church multiplication, one of Team Expansion's team leaders in North Africa had asked potential missionaries to get 100 prayer partners before joining his team and moving to the field. However, when the team leader learned that David Garrison listed "extraordinary prayer" as #1 of his "ten universals" (Garrison, Church Planting Movements, 2004, p. 33) in every church multiplication movement, the Team Expansion leader went back to the drawing board. In December 2010, he and his team set the goal to raise up 10,000 intercessors by the end of 2011. Just a couple of weeks later something extraordinary happened. There was a major demonstration in the downtown square. The next thing we knew, a revolution was shaking the country's government. The dictator went

Photo 11: A new day has arrived for CPM/DMM. It all starts with prayer.

into exile in a foreign land. The new government immediately went to work crafting a new constitution. The result was nothing short of amazing. Although the new constitution continued to recognize Islam as the official state religion, it also aspired to protect the beliefs and practices of other religions as well. Prayer did something that no politician could ever accomplish.

The goal of 10,000 intercessors had seemed impossible, but God worked and by December 31, 2011 there were almost 20,000 intercessors. They eventually hit the 100,000 mark (100,000 people praying every day for their focus nation), and God continued to move in power.

A new day has arrived. It all started with prayer. So should we.

(Note: The above text was provided by members of the actual team in North Africa. We aren't mentioning their names or their nation because of security.)

Questions for Discussion:

1. If Jesus wants all people to be saved, why do you think prayer seems to be a universal element in launching disciple-making movements? Why do you think God seemingly waits on us to pray?
2. How might we motivate believers to understand the potential power behind prayer? How could you do so for the initiatives that you are imagining for the church you attend or the place where you hope to make disciples?
3. If you were asked to pray for an unreached people group, never before engaged with the Good News, what would be some of your requests to God?
4. Take a moment to look up an unreached people group at www. JoshuaProject.net. Read about their needs and the opportunities for the Good News to spread there. Now take a few minutes actually to put into practice the concept of praying for the people about whom you're reading.

CHAPTER 5

OBEDIENCE AS THE COMMAND

Somehow, down through the years, in the Global North, we began equating church attendance with being a Christian. "Have you noticed how active she is? She's here every time the doors are open."

It's true that the Bible says not to forsake assembling together (Hebrews 10:25). On the other hand, James 1:22 says something just as important: "Do not merely listen to the word, and so deceive yourselves. Do what it says."

So obedience is hard-wired into the gospel. Jesus didn't tell His apostles to make disciples of all nations and teach them. Jesus instructed them to teach them **to obey** everything he had commanded them to do (Matthew 28:19-20). From the very beginning, we were supposed to be focused on training people to **obey**, not just **attend**.

But why should we be surprised that the emphasis has been on listening since the standard Western mindset is sitting and listening. As a result, we seem more focused on acquiring content instead of putting it into practice. In most churches, there's little, if any chance to give feedback or share lessons learned.

There's a lot of emphasis on the sermon but not on how to transform the lives of people who aren't attending our church. So we build attractional models. We encourage our members to invite someone to church in hopes that our visitors will decide to accept Christ. Since many sermons are designed for existing believers to grow deeper in the Word, visitors are left to wonder what THEY are supposed to do.

Having said all that, the fact that you're reading this book likely means that someone did a great job leading you to Christ. Odds are, somehow, the system worked for you. The fact that 1/3 of the world's inhabitants are at least nominal Christians is an awesome tribute to the power of God working through imperfect vessels. We give Him praise that, even though we can misunderstand clear commands in His Word, He can still work wonders through us.

So what should the church be like? **The church is like a spiritual family - followers of Jesus who love God, love people, and make disciples. Church members who meet together locally make up this last kind of church, the church at home (the simple church).** When groups of these simple churches connect to do something bigger, together, **they can form a city or regional church**. All of those simple churches networked into regions and stretched across history make up the universal Church. That's Church with a capital "C."

- Simple churches are spiritual families with Jesus as their center and their King.
- Simple churches are spiritual families who love God, love others, and make disciples who multiply.
- Some churches have buildings, programs, budgets, and staff.
- But simple churches don't need any of these things in order to love God, love others, and make disciples who multiply.

And since anything extra makes a church more complicated and harder to multiply, CPM/DMM training leaves things like buildings, programs, budgets, and staff to the city or regional church built from multiplying simple churches.

But before we start multiplying - let's make sure we know what God wants reproduced. Because multiplication can be good - but not always.

Cancer is multiplication. It's deadly. So how do we reproduce life and not death? How do we make sure we're disciples worth reproducing?

In CPM/DMM strategy and practice, the proof of the pudding is in the obedience. As Jerry Trousdale wrote in *The Kingdom Unleashed*,

> Many Christians in the Global North seem to think that transformation is a purely internal matter, accomplished through studying the Scriptures and perhaps through prayer. This reflects the knowledge-based model of discipleship common in Global North evangelicalism. We certainly don't intend to downplay the importance of studying and meditating on Scripture – but it is equally important to obey it. When Jesus discusses the last judgment, He does not tell us that He will judge us based on whether we pass a Scripture quiz; He tells us that He judges us based on how we live our life (Trousdale, 2018, pp. 317-318).

Photo 12: Simple churches of 4-12 people are a great environment for implementing love and obedience.

Jesus said, in John 13:35, "By this all men will know that you are My disciples, if you love one another." He added in John 14:15, "If you love Me, you will keep My commandments." He built on this topic even more in John 14:23, "Jesus replied, "If anyone loves Me, he will keep My word. My Father will love him, and we will come to him and make Our home with him."

These practices or habits, loving and obeying, are tough to acquire in an academic setting. They have to be lived out, modeled, talked through, and debriefed.

Churches of hundreds or thousands make accountability difficult. The "simple churches" of DMM, groups of 4-12 people, are a great environment for implementing love and obedience.

Spiritual Breathing

Some trainers have compared obedience to breathing perhaps because God calls His Spirit - "breath."

In the Kingdom, we breathe in when we hear from God (Zume-Project, Session 3). We breathe in when we hear from God through His Word, the Bible. We breathe in when we hear from God through prayer, our conversations with Him. We breathe in when we hear from God through His body, other followers of Jesus. We breathe in when we hear from God through His works, the experiences, and even the persecutions and sufferings He allows His children to go through.

In the Kingdom, we breathe out when we act on what we hear from God. We breathe out when we obey.

Sometimes breathing out to obey means changing our thoughts, our words, or our actions to bring them into alignment with Jesus and His will. Sometimes breathing out to obey means sharing what Jesus has shared with us - giving away what He gave us to bless others, just as God blesses us.

For a follower of Jesus, this breathing in and breathing out is critical. It's our very life. Jesus said - the Son can do nothing by himself. He does only what he sees the Father doing.

Jesus said that His followers would also hear from God because of His Holy Spirit - His Breath - that would be breathed into every one who follows Him. He explained that the Holy Spirit would teach His followers all things and remind them of everything He told us.

So when we hear from God, we are breathing in. When we obey what we hear and share it with others, we are breathing out. Jesus was showing us how to live.

So how do we hear God's voice? How do we know what to obey? In John 10:11, Jesus called Himself the Good Shepherd. Jesus called His followers His sheep. Jesus said in John 10:27, "My sheep hear my voice, and I know them, and they follow me." He also said, "Whoever belongs to God hears what God says. The reason you do not hear is that you do not belong to God" (John 8:47). As followers of Jesus, we have to be committed to hearing His voice.

- We hear His voice by being still.
- We hear His voice by focusing on Jesus.
- We hear His voice in our thoughts, our visions, our feelings, and impressions.
- We hear His voice when we write down and test what we hear.

Not every voice, not every thought, not every vision, feeling, or impression is God's voice. Sometimes it is the voice of the enemy. Jesus said our enemy is a liar and the father of lies. Jesus said our enemy comes to steal, kill, and destroy. God says that we will hear from Him. We will know it is He when He speaks. With practice and prayer, we can know God's voice better. We can learn to know whether what we hear is from God or another voice. Here are some ways to test what we hear:

- When Jesus speaks, His voice will always be consistent with what His written word, the Bible, has already told us. His spoken voice will never contradict His written voice.

- When Jesus speaks, His voice will give our hearts a sense of hope and peace. His voice will not leave us condemned or discouraged. Jesus does not condemn. Jesus corrects in love.
- Jesus's voice will not express the works of the flesh - sexual immorality and impurity, debauchery, idolatry and witchcraft, hatred and discord, jealousy and fits of rage, selfish ambitions, dissensions, factions and envy, drunkenness and orgies. These things are not from God's voice.
- When Jesus speaks - His voice will express the fruit of God's Spirit: love, joy, peace, patience, kindness, goodness, faithfulness, gentleness, and self-control.
- When Jesus speaks - His voice gives us a sense of confidence instead of doubt. We experience inside ourselves a knowledge and peace that what we're hearing is from God. We may not hear everything at once. We may hear only part of what we eventually will need to know. However, what we hear will be solid - not shifting or changing.

The good news for every follower of Jesus is that when we breathe in and hear from God and when we breathe out and obey what we hear and share with others what we've heard - God will speak even more clearly. His breath will breathe through us even more. We will hear His voice more clearly. We will know His voice and not another's. We will see His work in the world and be able to join in and work with Him. We breathe in. We breathe out.

In *The Kingdom Unleashed*, Trousdale tells of a street vendor he calls "Zahra" in a major city in one of the world's most intensely Muslim countries. She was introduced to CPM/DMM type initiatives in early 2016 "and eventually surrendered her life to Jesus. After that, she moved to the north of her country to be near her family and then set about learning to read well enough so that she could easily share any part of the Bible" (Trousdale, 2018, pp. 221-222).

He goes on to say,

She even started developing her own biblical story sets for different people and situations because she wanted all of the Discovery Bible Groups that were forming to learn to follow and obey God in any situation. She was starting groups when she was just six months into her time in the Lord. One of the women who discipled Zahra said in the interview that when they were doing traditional study groups, they had focused on converts, but in CPM/DMM studies, they focus on making **disciples**. The difference is their obedience, and that they have trust in God, not in us – they have crazy experiences with God that we can't even dream of.

Zahra had been separated from her husband for fifteen years. In one Bible study, the obedience element that she got from the passage was to choose to love her estranged husband, and she began to cry because she was still so bitter. Trousdale writes,

With tears in her eyes, she went to reconcile with her husband in the city where he lived. Now they are together again, and she commutes because of her work selling products on the street. And since reconciling with her husband, her business has improved. She had one hour when she sold her whole inventory – making as much money as she typically earned in a whole month before she was saved.

Zahra said, "This blessing is the glory of Jesus because I obeyed Him..."

The groups that Zahra catalyzed are now at three generations – in a place where every new group has to learn how to avoid the secret police and still multiply. Zahra shows the incredible things that average people can do when they are given the tools, coaching, and mentoring that they need as they need it. If churches in the Global North are going to see movements like we see in the

Global South, we will also need to provide training, mentorship, and permission to ordinary people to advance the Kingdom.

What's more, obedience is the ultimate and only way to respect God's infinite authority and power. He has all authority — and with that authority, He commanded us to make disciples. Re-read Matthew 28, but this time, start one verse earlier. Begin with verse 18 instead of 19. We say we have faith in Him. When we obey Him who gives a command, we are saying, I surrender to You, to Your will, to Your authority and power. At the end of the day, works don't save us in the least. Our obedience is indeed foundational to our saving faith because it shows our love for Him as a Savior and respect for His authority.

Photo 13: Obedience, in and of itself doesn't save. It shows our love and respect for Him.

Questions for Discussion:

1. Describe a church you have previously attended. (It could be your home church or the one you attend now.) In what ways do you feel this church has emphasized knowledge and attendance? In what ways has this church emphasized obedience and accountability?

2. Now that you've read this chapter, if it were up to you to design the perfect church, how might you recommend that we do church differently? (Note: Please avoid "trashing the bride of Christ." Please give respect to the church leaders who have gone before us and have done the best they can with what they understood.)

3. Have you seen churches which have emphasized teaching knowledge more than requiring obedience? If so, in your opinion, what is the root cause for this behavior?

4. This chapter compared obedience to breathing. What was difficult or helpful for you in looking at obedience in this way? If possible, explain your answer by giving an example?

5. This chapter opens the door to the concept that we might hear God's voice in the present rather than merely in the past. Is this concept troubling or encouraging to you? Do you agree or disagree with the idea?

CHAPTER 6

DISCOVERY-BASED LEARNING AS THE METHOD

Interestingly, even though these movements have arisen on different continents through the hands of a wide spectrum of trainers, most all of them have at least this one factor in common: They all end up having to rely on discovery-based learning rather than lecture-format teaching. When you stop and consider, it should come as no surprise why this has happened. First, most all these movements do originate from a common strand of DNA that can be traced back to a fairly small group of trainers and friends. So obviously, the common origins have begotten some common practices; however, there is a second, more practical reason. Any other solution (e.g., lecture-format teaching) would presumably have to rely on trained teachers instructing these waves of new believers and, try as they might, the fast-growing movements we're seeing just wouldn't have time to train leaders at the pace required to keep step with the growth. No, the only way to keep pace is for the group to generate its own learning system. A discovery-based learning system fits the bill. Why is that?

When reading and studying a Bible passage, discovery-based learning focuses on a set of questions — usually something along the lines of...

1. What did you like about this passage?

2. What did you find difficult about this passage? (What didn't you understand?)
3. What does this passage teach you about people?
4. What does this passage teach you about God/Jesus?
5. How will you obey this passage?
6. Who will you train with this message?
7. With whom will you share your story or the story of God?

These seven questions (or questions very similar to them) make up the pivotal core of what many CPM/DMM trainers call a Discovery Bible Study or DBS. Some have customized the name to emphasize certain characteristics or unique practices (DBS, Life Conversation Group, "three-thirds group," and more), but at least the core of the study seems to have a lot in common, and discovery-based learning is the core of the core. Because this study incorporates a bit more than a Bible study and because it's so different from a classical Bible study as we know it, in this book, we prefer using the term, "three-thirds group" (or 3/3 group) to help learners understand that this is not your typical Bible study. A 3/3 group, then, is a gathering of 4-12 people who want to learn to love God, love others, and make disciples. They "do life" together in their three-thirds group, holding one another accountable to goals that they, themselves, set, in response to hearing God's Word and applying it. The name comes from the fact that the study consists of three "thirds" – a look back (at the past week), a look up (at what God has said in a portion of His Word), and a look forward (at goals for the coming week). A three-thirds group essentially can be a "simple church," either standing on its own, or within the context of a larger "city church" or "regional church network."

Now you might be asking, "How can a bunch of questions elicit any kind of content that's worth hearing?" It's kind of hard to explain, but this approach somehow works in a powerful way. This group interaction with the passage, inspired directly by the Holy Spirit, brings out so many insights. It also elevates the Word and gives the Bible the highest regard because, instead of focusing on an outline developed by a preacher, the group is focusing totally on the outline in Scripture. LeRoy Eims was a very-early proponent of this kind of approach. He wrote in his prophetic book, *The Lost Art of Disciple Making* (Eims, 1978),

> [Christians] may be surrounded by Bibles in their homes, but if something should happen to the pastor or church so that there was no Sunday morning preaching service, they would go without their spiritual food. They would have no nourishment for their souls. If someone is not available to break open the Word of God and feed them, they would go hungry. The problem is not that there is no spiritual food. The problem is that many Christians do not know how to get it for themselves. They are like babies in a pantry surrounded by all kinds of canned goods - meats, fruits, vegetables. But they would starve to death unless someone opened those cans for them (p. 53).

But there's another benefit. Because there is no real "leader" exactly (only a group **facilitator**), everyone feels positioned as an equal. What this means is that it no longer matters if one of the group members has a degree from a seminary, while another member has just opened the Bible for the first time ever. The Bible is the revealed word of God. It's powerful enough to speak on its own. At the same time, this helps lay the groundwork for group members turning into group starters. It also helps newcomers feel welcome to participate. Furthermore, by participating, we engage more with the passage than we would if we were merely hearing about it. What's more, even the absolute first-timer brings fresh perspective and, in fact, finds hope in the Scripture. Beyond all this, our common sense tells us that the more we can stay engaged with learning, the more interesting learning will be.

There might be another reason why discovery-based learning is working so well in these movements. We all enjoy discovering something on our own. When we uncover a truth, especially if the group affirms it in the passage, we feel as if we've found a diamond or struck an oil well. We probably will remember it better (than if someone else merely **told** us about it). Studies from the past couple of decades have shown again and again that lecture-based models (similar to the typical sermons taking place in most of our churches in the current day) can be somewhat effective. Active learning, incorporating the use of questions and personal application, is radically more effective in every way (Brame). In fact, one study found that students in a lecture-based class were 55% more likely to fail than similar students in a class which incorporated active learning methods, including asking questions, analyzing content, and formulating theories on meanings (Freeman, Active learning increases student performance in science, engineering, and mathematics, 2014). The seven questions asked in a discovery Bible study help us apply what we learn, connecting ideas with actions. We stay engaged, our mind has to focus, and we find it easier to tell someone else about what we studied.

Now we know it's easy to scoff at this and say, "This isn't biblical." Right. Cultures vary profoundly, so how can one learning approach have ever become so popular in a particular style of group multiplication? Right. All those criticisms and many more could be leveled. Here's an equally profound conclusion (please hear this with an open mind): Hundreds of thousands (maybe millions?) of new believers have demonstrated the ability to learn this simple approach (discovery-based Scripture

learning) then rapidly replicate it among others. In many cases, they've shared it rapidly with non-believers. Go back and re-read Chapter 3 ("Disciple-making Works") and ponder the fact that most of those case studies utilized some form of discovery-based learning/ training as a primary form

Photo 14: Discovery Bible Studies (three-thirds groups) have proven to be wildly effective in many parts of the world.

of multiplication. Our conclusion, after examining scores of these case studies, is that God seems to be using this approach in our day to grow His church and expand His Kingdom in wildly effective examples. It's true that discovery-based learning isn't the **only** way to study the Bible; but we heartily recommend that learners try it, if for no other reason than to understand why it has been working so effectively throughout the rest of the world.

Discovery-Based Learning and Abram

Anecdotally, allow me to share this narrative example. In the spring of 2018, a friend contacted me from a large island in the Pacific (which we'll leave unnamed for the sake of security). On a recent Sunday morning, a Muslim refugee from the Middle East had visited his church asking for help in "finding out who Jesus is." My friend was in the middle of a very busy season of life. He would have **loved** to walk this visitor through a course of study, but he was over committed. My friend had been reading about my quest to learn more about CPM/DMM, so he asked me if I knew someone who might help. I was just curious enough to ask why someone from the Middle East might do such a thing — and besides, if it were at all true, I longed for this seeker to find truth, hope, help, and love in the Person he was seeking. A few short days later, I was talking to the young man via Skype. Let's call him Abram. Abram had been forced to flee his homeland because of war and because he had been caught on the wrong end of some political ideologies that resulted in a price being put on his head. In a nearby land, a believer there shared a Scripture portion with him in a printed booklet. Abram didn't remember exactly what the booklet (or the Scripture) said, but that night, he had a dream that a man in white handed him a glowing letter. When Abram opened the letter, it was signed by Jesus. He was now on a quest to find out who this Jesus was and what the letter might have meant. I told Abram that the letter might have represented the Bible and asked him if he would like to read it with me. He was as eager as anyone I had ever seen.

The Start Track: Inquiring Bible Students Want to Know

With deep respect, it was like someone from another planet had landed on earth. He started with very little foundation, yet he was absorbing everything so quickly. I followed standard CPM/DMM approaches with him (other than the fact that we were having to do all this over Skype or Zoom video-conference calls). We did a series of eight discovery Bible studies. (These 8 passages are a great way to begin with **any** inquirer. Some have referred to this as the "Start Track.") Those eight Scriptures were:

1. Mark 5:1-20 (During this study, Abram compared himself to the man with impure spirits. He instinctively wanted to find Jesus so the torment of his life would end.)
2. 1 Corinthians 15:1-8, Romans 3:23, Romans 6:23 (At the end of this study, Abram seemed to "get it." He already seemed to grasp that he needed to leave Islam and accept Jesus.)
3. Mark 1:16-20 (In this study, even though he hadn't fully accepted Christ yet, I asked him to make a list of all of the people who might be impacted by his decision. He messaged me later the same day, telling me he had 108 on his list so far.)
4. Romans 6:3-4, Acts 8:26-40 (Following this study, Abram started asking whether or not he could be baptized.)
5. 2 Timothy 3:14-16 (After this study, Abram began reading the Bible. In fact, he began devouring it. He said he wanted to read through the entire book before his baptism. Amazingly, that's exactly what he did.)
6. Matthew 6:9-13 (On this day, Abram prayed the most beautiful prayer ever, out loud, directly to God.)

Photo 15: After the fourth study, Abram started asking if he could be baptized. (Actual photo of Abram's baptism. Used with permission.)

7. Acts 5:17-42, Matthew 5:43-44 (During this session, Abram wept for his wife and children back home in the Middle East. He had begun to realize that he simply HAD to tell them about Jesus, even if it meant that he would be persecuted, jailed, or even killed. He asked about baptism again in this study. I asked the question, "Abram, are you so convinced that you want to be baptized that, even if it results in your death, you would still want to follow Jesus — no matter what?" His eyes filled with tears. He answered, after pondering just a moment, "Yes." We had done seven discovery Bible studies in a span of time equal to 14 days or so. Based on his answer, on this day, we began organizing for his baptism. It took a while, since the island in the Pacific has strict laws forbidding Muslim citizens from converting. Those who break those norms are often beaten and sometimes killed.)

8. Acts 2:42-47, 1 Corinthians 11:23-34 (In this study, it seemed like Abram fully captured what the community of Christ (the church) was supposed to be.)

At this point I asked him if he would like to learn how to share his faith with others so they could understand Jesus's Good News too. He eagerly said yes. I explained that we could begin a 10-week training called Zúme, designed to help him become a disciple worth multiplying and to train him how to multiply in others. He didn't even blink. He was eager to begin. I recruited a couple of others to do the study with him. We began Zúme without missing a beat, just a few days later. Keep in mind, the only kind of Bible study we had done so far had been discovery-based.

The Questions

We always used the same set of seven questions.

1. What did you like about this passage?

2. What did you find difficult about this passage? (What didn't you understand?)
3. What does this passage teach you about people?
4. What does this passage teach you about God/Jesus?
5. How will you obey this passage?
6. Who will you train with this message?
7. With whom will you share your story or the story of God?

The seventh session of Zúme presents these questions as the preferred outline for Bible study. During that session, Abram quipped, "You know, when they study the Bible at my friend's church, they do it differently." Abram continued, "When you and I study the Bible, we try to understand what the Bible is saying. You ask questions. You even listen to my answers. I'm just a beginner. But when you listen to my answers, it encourages me. You treat me with respect, even if you have to point me back to the verses to help me see the meaning. You could just tell me what I'm supposed to believe. But somehow, when you ask questions and I have to think about the answers, it makes it more interesting. I get to talk more. And I think I learn more, too." He had already recognized intuitively what we were learning experientially: We learn more through discovery than just about any other method around.

New Life

Abram was baptized following the fourth Zúme study. By the time Abram finished all the sessions of Zúme, he had already shared his faith with a dozen people — no small accomplishment in a country in which proselytization is legally forbidden. No **wonder** there are 651 movements worldwide. Discovery-based learning is only a piece of the overall strategy. However, it's an important piece.

Questions for Discussion:

1. Assess why discovery-based learning might provide a better solution for training leaders in a fast-growing movement? Has your church or organization tried to use this approach? If not, venture guesses as to why not.

2. Some have said that utilizing the same set of questions about each new Bible passage would become formulaic (the pattern would "get old" or become too mechanical rather quickly). Do you agree or disagree?

3. What would it mean to you to study the Bible using discovery-based learning? Would you feel you were somehow "missing out" on the insights of a great teacher that you respect or know? Explain.

4. You've probably heard before that "active learning" increases our chances of retaining information. Yet, would you agree or disagree – most churches have retained the form of teaching known as "the sermon." Offer some best guesses about why the church has retained this approach down through the centuries. Does it create a moral dilemma for you to ponder the possibility of transforming this approach to a new paradigm?

5. For you personally, does it bother you that discovery-based learning isn't mentioned per se in the Bible?

CHAPTER 7

PEER ACCOUNTABILITY

Many of us have been involved with Bible studies down through the years. We've participated in life groups, adult Bible fellowships, Sunday School, and many other small gatherings. We might have even visited something similar to a discovery Bible study. So why are THESE discovery Bible studies producing such incredible growth? One of the major reasons is the action orientation spurred on by peer accountability. At the close of the discovery Bible study, we ask three critical questions:

- How will you obey this passage?
- Whom will you train with this message?
- With whom will you share your story or the story of God?

The group facilitator essentially looks everyone in the eye, one by one, prompting each participant to provide a real name in answer to the last two questions. CPM/DMM trainers apologetically point out that many of us are spurred on to good works when we know that others in our circle are waiting to see what we will tackle. It's not that we want to look good (pride). It's that we don't want to be BAD (disobedience). Some facilitators will make a chart (see Table 1) with the names of the group members across the top and key words for the three questions down the side. In the chart, the group records its answers, which become, in a way, a goal or a plan for the coming week. Facilitators will often email, text, or use some kind of collaboration software to share this chart with others in the group a couple of days later as a reminder of their personal commitments. Remember, these are self-directed goals. No one is handing out assignments. Group members are held to their own spiritual "next steps" only after God has personally prompted them to the calling that He, Himself, gives them after a time of prayer at the end of each week's session.

This peer accountability factor is of the utmost importance. After everyone answers these three questions, the group divides up into pairs or three's, then practices one or more of the conversations. The group is basically role-playing the way they hope to approach their friend or colleague. The buddy is listening and role-playing the response. The group then ends with focused prayer for the obey, train, and sharing.

Table 1: Example goals from a three-thirds group.

Mk 5:1-20	Simon	Doug	Ryan	Abram
5: Obey	Be more alert to opportunities God creates	Be more open to the Spirit's prompting	Look for those in need	Tell those in my homeland about Jesus
6. Train	Mohammed	Leo	Roommate	Atil
7. Share	Peter	Mike	Landlord	Noor

When group members receive the message with the above chart, they realize that everyone else in the group is seeing their commitment. Hopefully, the group members pray for one another throughout the week, with a goal that each participant will follow through.

But there's still something special about knowing the day of the meeting is approaching. We all live in such a hurry, it's so easy to get lost in the events of the week, lose track of time, and not follow through. However, as the day approaches, I end up **making** time. Why? Because I have made a commitment with my fellow group members. I don't want to destroy the trust that we have worked hard to build. So, because of this peer accountability, I will often push myself to keep my commitment because I know at the beginning of the upcoming study, there is a time of reviewing how we did. The facilitator might ask, "So how did it go this past week?"

In a typical Bible study that is focused on content/knowledge, some participants hide "under the radar." In one of these groups, with peer accountability, it's pretty impossible to hide out. So what happens to the people who don't really want to obey/implement? They typically self-select out of the group after a few weeks. Furthermore, maybe they should. In a CPM/DMM approach, we want to encourage members who are willing and able to implement. Peer accountability acts as a kind of filter to find and encourage those people.

Is peer accountability mentioned in the Bible? Not exactly. Does that mean it won't work? Go re-read the Case Studies in Chapter 3 again and judge for yourself. By the way, calendars aren't mentioned in the New Testament either. Neither are to do lists, nor iPhones — and many of us use those, too. In Romans, Paul writes of his next step plans.

But now I no longer have any work to do in these provinces, and I have strongly desired for many years to come to you whenever I travel to Spain. For I hope to see you when I pass through, and to be assisted by you for my journey there, once I have first enjoyed your company for a while. Right now I am traveling to Jerusalem to serve the saints... So when I have finished this and safely delivered the funds to them, I will visit you on the way to Spain.... (Romans 15:23-29).

Peer accountability is as useful as (maybe more useful than) a task list or a calendar. It's consistent with Paul's written plan in Romans 15; God is using it in a mighty way to multiply disciples and groups worldwide.

Questions for Discussion:

1. Perhaps you've already participated in a Bible study in which you were held accountable to make decisions about your actions then follow through with them. (If not, then try to imagine it.) Does it – or would it – annoy you to have someone ask you, the following week, if you followed through? Explain.

2. The author held that accountability works not because we want to look good (pride), but rather, because we don't want to look bad (disobedience). Do you agree or disagree? Explain.

3. This chapter gave some very practical ways to implement accountability at the close of a Bible study. Analyze for your life – does this concept seem too rigid or cult-like to you? Why or why not?

4. This chapter provided an example of a Bible figure sharing his plans or next steps prior to implementing them. Do you agree or disagree that this is an example of peer accountability? Why or why not?

CHAPTER 8

MULTIPLYING GROUPS

There's another background issue that is fundamental to movements. It's much less tangible and more subjective — but it's just as "core" as the ideas above. If we're going to see multiplication happen, we have to transform our thinking about "additions." We have to start thinking in terms of multiplying **groups**.

Robert M. Reach has written about this idea:

If a church fills a 5,000-seat sanctuary multiple times over an Easter weekend, somebody will write an article about it. ... Of course, addition is better than no growth at all. But if you assume that movement growth happens by adding individuals to established churches that are growing like an inflating balloon, you will have trouble imagining what is actually happening. Movements work differently (Reach, 2016, p. 26).

Perhaps this is one of the reasons that there are relatively few movements so far being identified in the Global North. We already have an established paradigm of churches. These churches already have established benchmarks. They measure success by addition. With these existing benchmarks and dashboards, perhaps we can't think outside the box. "The box," is — church as we know it; addition as we have known it; growth as we have known it. Movements work differently.

Reach adds, "We must move beyond our church-growth expectations of bigger is best. Movements hold networks of organic simple churches that usually meet in a home, a village hut or a common place in a small town" (Reach, 2016, p. 27).

Unfortunately, the transition is tough. Again, perhaps that's why "hybrid" churches are rare. Neil Cole explains, "We can't start with addition and end with multiplication. We cannot pretend that the methods of incremental growth we employ will result in exponential impact" (Cole, 2010).

Part of Two Churches

Still, CPM/DMM thinking begins expanding our paradigms when it comes to groups anyway. In the CPM/DMM way of thinking, in God's Word - we learn that His perfect plan is for us to live as a spiritual family. The Bible talks about this family as a church in three forms (ZumeProject, Session 9):

- The universal Church - all the followers of Jesus from all time periods and all places make up this church.
- The regional or city church - the gathering of all the believers in a city or a part of a country.
- The simple church - the gathering of believers who meet in a small group like in a building or a home.

This smallest group, the "simple church," is the spiritual family that lives life together and it works best when that family can meet and work together for months or years at a time. At the same time, Jesus instructed His followers that they should be continuously starting new spiritual families, growing them to be more like Jesus, and helping them learn how to start new spiritual families, too. Jesus told us, "Therefore go and make disciples of all nations, baptizing them in the name of the Father and of the Son and of the Holy Spirit, and teaching them to obey everything I have commanded you" (Matthew 28:19-20). So how do these two things come together - how can we be a part of a church and be in the process of starting new churches - all at the same time?

Imagine a basic church - just four families. Each family leads and lives life in their own home. Each family is also part of one church. This is their ongoing spiritual family. This is who they do life with - the brothers and sisters who encourage them in love and good works.

Photo 16: Imagine a "simple church" (home group) whose members were always trying to multiply their group.

But these same couples are also each working to start a new spiritual family. They're not participating in the same way they do with their own small group family, but they help by modeling and assisting a new spiritual family until it can get started and grow to a point that it can stand on its own. Imagine if each of the four couples could do this separately — or even in pairs. In this way, while they are doing church together as one "spiritual family," they would also be launching four (or two) other new spiritual families simultaneously. This is how fast God can grow His family. This is how the church can increase its pace.

Most people will not be able to help launch more than one other new spiritual family at a time. However, they might be able to learn to watch over and coach multiple churches and help them connect with peer mentors as they grow. That means one single spiritual family - one small group church - can be part of launching many other small group churches at exactly the same time. That could expand exponentially our capacity as a global church to reach the lost. What's more, we would see a lot more fruit than ever before. New believers would all have their **own** spiritual families which they could home.

So what happens to all these churches as they grow and start new churches that start new churches that start new churches? How do they stay connected? How do they live life as an extended spiritual family? The answer is that all of these simple churches are just like the cells in a growing body and they connect together and network into a city or regional church. The churches are related. They share the same spiritual DNA. They are all connected out of the same first multiplying family. Consequently, with some guidance, they come together as a larger body to do even more.

CPM/DMM training helps expand our mind in the area of multiplying groups. If churches (as we have always defined them) have focused on attracting people to a building, then perhaps what we need to do is expand our thinking by trying to attract people primarily to the Bible. So, with this shift, we would no longer be inviting people primarily to a church. We'd be inviting them to our houses, our meetings, our **groups, and the Bible** — so they could personally encounter Jesus. That's a shift for the Global North. The question church leaders have to ask is — are you willing to make that shift?

Questions for Discussion:

1. This chapter doesn't criticize a church for meeting in large gatherings. Rather, it points to a way forward that focuses on multiplication rather than addition. Can you think of an example of this in a church or campus ministry that you've attended? How might multiplication be a help?

2. Think hard about your own life. This chapter speaks of regularly being part of two churches – one church or group for our own spiritual worship and a second church or group that we're

helping launch. Ponder this thought for your own life. What would it take for you to implement this concept?

3. Evaluate the effectiveness of a church or group that you've attended compared to the paradigm presented in this chapter. Compare and contrast.

4. Assume for a moment that multiplication is the best way forward. How might we help the church at large to grasp this paradigm and do it?

CHAPTER 9

MAXIMIZING FRUIT

CPM/DMM trainers often speak of helping new disciples transition from being consumers to producers. In His perfect plan, God created us to live in balance - to **produce** and to **consume**, to **create** and to **use up**, to **pour out** and to be **filled** so we can **pour out** again. Unfortunately, in our broken world, people have rejected God's plan, and many spend their energy living out just part of God's perfect equation. They **learn,** but they don't share. They are **filled up,** but they never pour out. They **consume,** but they don't produce. If we're going to make disciples who multiply, then we need to share with them how they can be producers and not just consumers. Here are some practices that can help.

Self-feeding in the Word

In CPM/DMM approaches, the Bible is lifted up as the highest authority. God uses His written Word (the Bible) to grow us spiritually (ZumeProject, Session 2). Every disciple needs to be equipped to learn, interpret, and apply Scripture. Over thousands of years and through many different authors, God spoke His word into the hearts of faithful men who captured and shared what they heard. The Scriptures teach us God's story, His plans, His heart, His ways. CPM/DMM trainers often teach three tools, listed and explained below:

- SOAPS Bible Study
- Accountability Groups
- 3/3 Groups

These three tools work together to help equip new followers to learn, interpret, and apply God's written Word. They will learn how to be doers and sharers of what they hear from God's Word.

Let's look at each of the three tools in closer detail.

SOAPS Bible Study

First, what do we mean when we say "SOAPS Bible Study" (ZumeProject Session 1)?

Jesus said, "Therefore go and make disciples of all nations, baptizing them in the name of the Father and of the Son and of the Holy Spirit, and teaching them to obey everything I have commanded you" (Matthew 28:19-20). If every follower of Jesus is going to obey all that Jesus commanded, then he or she needs to know what Jesus commands. The Great Commandment and The Great Commission are a great summary of what God has to say to us; but if a follower is going to grow into the full measure of what God created them to be, then he or she needs to know and obey even more.

CPM/DMM trainers encourage us to study the Bible for ourselves every day. SOAPS becomes a great tool for us to use when doing that. SOAPS stands for:

- Scripture
- Observation
- Application
- Prayer
- Sharing

It's a simple way to learn and remember an effective

Photo 17: SOAPS is a simple way to learn and remember an effective Bible study method.

Bible study method that any follower of Jesus can use. Let's look at each section a little more.

When you read or listen to the Bible, try using this style of Bible study:

- Scripture: Write out one or more verses that are particularly meaningful to you, today.
- Observation: Rewrite those verses or key points from those Scriptures in your own words to help you better understand the meaning.
- Application: Think about what it means to obey these commands or concepts in your own life. What would you have to do? What would you have to do differently? Write these down.
- Prayer: Write out a prayer that tells God what you've read in His Word and what you understand about obeying His commands and putting what you've learned to work.
- Sharing: Ask God who He wants you to share with about what you've learned and how you're applying it.

So let's put SOAPS to work by using an example:

- Scripture: Suppose you were reading in the 55th chapter of the book of Isaiah. There, you come across the verse, "For my thoughts are not your thoughts, nor are your ways My ways," declares the Lord. "For as the heavens are higher than the earth, so are My ways higher than your ways and My thoughts than your thoughts" (Isaiah 55:8-9).
- Observation: Your observation might be, "I'm limited in what I know and what I know how to do. God is not limited in any way. He sees and knows everything. He can do anything."
- Application: As you seek to apply this passage, you might reason, "Since God knows everything and His ways are best, I'll have much more success in life if I follow Him instead of relying on my way of doing things."

- Prayer: You could pray, "Lord, I don't know how to live a good life that pleases you and helps others. My ways lead to mistakes. My thoughts lead to hurt. Please teach me Your ways and Your thoughts instead. Let Your Holy Spirit guide me as I follow You."
- Sharing: This might prompt you to conclude, "I will share these verses and this application with my friend, Steve, who is going through a difficult time and needs direction for important decisions he's facing."

To summarize, doing a SOAPS-style study is not the **only** way to study the Bible. However, if we each studied the Bible in this way every day, we would all learn a lot more about God's Word AND, together, as a church, we would be more engaged in "self-feeding" instead of having to depend on others to teach us the Bible. Remember, SOAPS isn't something we do as a group in a weekly study. It's something we're encouraged to do daily, on our own, independently. We don't have to use the same Scripture passages (though that works great, too). We **do** have to do **something** to stay in the Word.

Accountability Groups

Second, what do we mean by accountability groups (ZumeProject, Session 1)? Jesus said, "From everyone who has been given much, much will be demanded; and from the one who has been entrusted with much, much more will be asked" (Luke 12:48b). Jesus shared many stories of accountability and told us many truths of how we will be held responsible for what we do and say. Jesus tells us these things now, so we can be ready for later. Because we will be accountable to Him one day, it's good to practice being accountable to one another now.

Accountability groups are made up of two or three people of the same gender - men with men, women with women - who meet once a week to pray and discuss a set of questions that help reveal areas where things are going right and other areas that need correction.

What kinds of questions should an accountability group partner ask? Here are a couple of different sets of questions from which accountability partners could choose. You could do all the questions or as many as time allows, then start next time where you left off.

List 1:

- How are you doing?
- How is your prayer life?
- Do you have any sin to confess? (Relational, Sexual, Financial, Pride, Integrity, Submission to Authority, etc.)
- Did you obey what God told you last time? Share details.
- Did you pray for the "Unbelievers" on your relationship list this week?
- Did you have the chance to share with any of them? Share details.
- Did you memorize a new verse this week? Quote it.
- Did you read at least 25 chapters in the Bible this week?
- What did God say to you this week from the Word?
- What are you going to specifically do about it?
- Did you meet with your 3/3 group this week? How did it go?
- Did you model or assist someone in starting a new 3/3 group this week? Share details.
- Do you see anything hindering my walk with Christ?
- Did you have the opportunity to share the gospel this week? Share details.
- Who can you invite to the accountability group next week? If the group is four or more, multiply it.

List 2:

- How have your insights from last week's reading shaped the way you think and live?

- Who did you pass your insights from last week on to and how was it received?
- How have you seen God at work?
- Have you been a testimony this week to the greatness of Jesus Christ with both your words and actions?
- Have you been exposed to sexually alluring material or allowed your mind to entertain inappropriate sexual thoughts?
- Have you acknowledged God's ownership in your use of money?
- Have you coveted anything?
- Have you hurt someone's reputation or feelings by your words?
- Have you been dishonest in word or action or exaggerated?
- Have you given into an addictive (or lazy or undisciplined) behavior?
- Have you been a slave to clothing, friends, work, or possessions?
- Have you failed to forgive someone?
- What worries or anxieties are you facing? Have you complained or grumbled?
- Have you maintained a thankful heart?

Photo 18 : Accountability groups are made up of 2 or 3 individuals of the same gender.

- Have you been honoring, understanding, and generous in your important relationships?
- What temptations in thought, word, or action have you faced and how did you respond?
- How have you taken opportunities to serve or bless others, especially believers?
- Have you seen specific answers to prayer?
- Did you complete the reading for the week?

3/3 Group

Jesus said, "For where two or three gather in my name, there am I with them" (Matthew 19:20). That's a powerful promise, and one that every follower of Jesus should claim. As a result, you might form or join a group in order to understand and apply scripture, care for group needs, and prepare for sharing the biblical life practices with others. When you come together in the group, how should you spend your time? A 3/3 Group (Note: Pronounce as "Three-Thirds") is one that divides its time together into 3 parts so that the group can practice obeying some of the most important things that Jesus commands. So what do the three thirds look like in detail?

The First Third (20 minutes or about 1/3 of your time together): First, a 3/3 group might open with some form of worship. The group might sing a couple of simple praise songs or even take communion together. The group then looks back at the previous week (or back to the previous meeting, whenever that was, assuming the group has met before). The facilitator might invite group members to share a brief story about how God revealed Himself in an unexpected way. Participants could also choose to share a prayer request, answer to prayer, or a praise. The group then prays for one another.

Next the facilitator moves the group into a series of questions that help build a relationship of accountability among the group members. The facilitator might ask, "How have you obeyed something that you learned from the prior lesson?" and/or "Whom have you trained in something that you have learned?" Afterward, the members might take turns sharing some kind of testimony – or if they've been practicing, they might rehearse telling God's story to the rest of the group. Group members are especially encouraged to give any examples of those who have come to faith and/or those who have been baptized. This is tremendous encouragement for the group.

The group closes this first third of the 3/3 group by recapping why they gather. In this "vision casting" time, they usually share a story from the Bible (like Matt. 28:18-20, Luke 10:1-11, Acts 1:8, Luke 19:1-10,

Matt. 13: 1-23, Luke 24:45-49), or they share an encouraging or inspirational story. This reminds the group when they gather. Because they recap this vision, they remember together how they are different from most all other typical Bible studies.

The Second Third (the second 20 minutes or about 1/3 of your time): To begin this section, the group members all turn to the scripture that the facilitator has chosen for the 3/3 group study. The facilitator asks if someone might be willing to read the passage after the group prays. Once someone agrees, a volunteer prays that God would teach the group about this week's passage. Immediately after the prayer, the volunteer reads the passage all the way through. (Note: Most groups discourage taking turns at reading various sections of the passage because this kind of reading can actually end up substantially disrupting the momentum of the reading. As a result, usually one person volunteers to read the entire passage. After the reading, the facilitator guides the discussion through the first two (of seven) questions.

1. What did you like about this passage?
2. What did you find difficult about this passage or what didn't you understand?

The facilitator tries to insure that everyone has a turn to speak and that no one dominates the conversation. And certainly, the facilitator protects the group from bullies or autocrats. After 10 minutes or so, or when discussion seems to be dying down, the facilitator asks for another reading. It's common that this second reading might be from a different version of the Bible. For example, if the first reader, above, used NIV, perhaps this second reading might be from New American Standard (or any other translation version that a group member has available). Following the second reading, the facilitator takes the group through 2 more questions.

3. What does this passage teach you about people?
4. What does this passage teach you about God/Jesus?

The Final Third: Look Forward (the last 20 minutes or so, or the last 1/3 of your time). In this last section of the group meeting, the facilitator asks group members to spend some time quietly asking God what He would have them say or do. Group members then each take turns answering three additional questions (always the same three):

5. How will you obey this passage?
6. Who will you train with this message?
7. With whom will you share your story or the story of God?

After sharing the answers to these three questions, the group members practice. They divide up (usually in pairs or groups of no more than two or three), then practice what they have committed to do when they each answered questions 5, 6, and 7. Members can role-play to make it real. They practice teaching the day's passage, or they might try sharing God's Story in the form of the 3 Circles tool. They might practice sharing their personal testimonies or telling the "Creation to Judgment Story." Afterward, they pray either in their practice pairs or as a full group. They ask God to prepare the hearts of the people who will be hearing about Jesus the coming week. They also ask Him for strength to be obedient to their commitments.

In the Appendix, you'll find a guidesheet for facilitating a 3/3 group in your home, neighborhood, or with your friends. Also, in the Zúme course, session 6, you can watch

Photo 19: In the Zúme course, you can learn exactly how to facilitate a great 3/3 group.

a 3/3 group in its entirety via video. Some might say, "Why should we **watch** a group? Shouldn't we just **do** a 3/3 group in our own study course?" The answer to that question might always be yes. There is great value in seeing a "model" group so everyone is on the same page and can effectively capture what occurs in a 3/3 group. Therefore, we recommend that **everyone** watch the example group in Session 6, then by any and all means, seek to launch or join a 3/3 group in your neighborhood or with your friends right away. By the way, we highly recommend you follow the guide sheet in the Appendix as closely as possible. This same approach has resulted in thousands of reproducing groups. Please don't be quick to throw any parts of it out the window indiscriminately.

The Appendix also contains a "Zúme Course Facilitator Guidesheet and Resources" sheet. Although that guide was prepared specifically for Zúme, it's also helpful for those facilitating 3/3 groups, too. There are several hints and suggestions there which apply perfectly to 3/3 groups in general. (It's kind of like a job description.) Of particular importance is the encouragement to multiply 3/3 groups and not just multiply trainings. When compared to long-term 3/3 groups, trainings, though valuable, are much less likely to contain the kind of accountability, heartfelt worship, and personal accountability. If we just multiply trainings (alone), are we really satisfying the long-term goal of making disciples? By contrast, 3/3 groups are designed for our spiritual growth long-term.

Self-feeding in Prayer

God also uses His Spoken Word - which we can discern through Prayer — to grow us spiritually (ZumeProject, Session 2). Prayer is speaking and listening to God. Prayer helps us know God more intimately and understand His heart, His will, and His ways. Prayer helps us minister and serve others, helps us teach and share in specific ways that help individuals or a group know God better. Two simple tools - Prayer Walking and The Prayer Cycle help followers develop personal prayer lives and learn to pray in ways that serve others. These tools help develop a habit of praying without ceasing and learning to see the world from a spiritual perspective instead of only relying on what we can visibly see. When used consistently, these tools help a follower of Jesus increase his capacity for prayer and enhance his ability to hear from God and share what he hears.

Let's first look more closely at **The Prayer Cycle** (ZumeProject, Session 2). Jesus often taught His followers about the purpose, the practice, and the promises of prayer. Jesus said, "Ask and it will be given to you; seek and you will find; knock and the door will be opened to you. For everyone who asks receives; the one who seeks finds; and to the one who knocks, the door will be opened" (Matthew 7:7-8).

Jesus taught His followers that prayer isn't for public praise, a selfish wish list, or a rambling speech we repeat over and over again. Jesus showed us prayer has power because it's a direct and ongoing conversation with our Father in heaven who loves us. Like any good conversation, a good prayer means both sides get to listen and speak. Except speaking to the God who created the universe can seem intimidating. Furthermore, actually hearing something back – well, for most people, that can be downright scary. The good news is that getting better at prayer - having better and deeper conversations with a God who loves us - is not only possible, it's exactly what God wants. When prayer feels like learning a new language, how do you get better? The answer is simple - you practice. The Prayer Cycle is a simple tool for practicing prayer that you can use by yourself and share with any follower. In just 12 simple steps of 5 minutes each, the Prayer Cycle guides us through multiple biblical ways to pray. At the end, you'll have prayed for an hour. The Bible tells us to pray continually (1 Thessalonians 5:17). Not many of us can say we do that. After an hour of prayer using The Prayer Cycle tool (see Figure 20. The Prayer Cycle), you'll be a step closer.

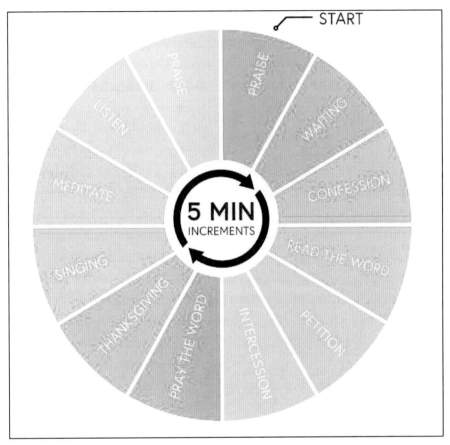

START

5 MIN
INCREMENTS

Figure 20. The Prayer Cycle

Next, let's look at **Prayer Walking**. This is a simple way to obey God's command to pray for others. Prayer walking is just what it sounds like - praying to God while walking around. Instead of closing our eyes and bowing our heads, we keep our eyes open to the needs we see around us and bow our hearts to ask humbly for God to intervene. You can prayer walk in small groups of two or three or you can prayer walk by yourself. If you go in a group, try having everyone pray out loud, a conversation with God about what everyone is seeing and the needs that God brings to their hearts. If you go by yourself, pray silently or out loud if you pray with someone you meet along the way. Here are four ways you can know what to pray for during your prayer walk:

1. Observation: What do you see? If you see a child's toy in a yard, you might be prompted to pray for the neighborhood's children, for families, or for schools in the area.
2. Research: What do you know? If you've read up about the neighborhood, you might know something about the people who live there, or if the area suffers from crime or injustice. Pray about these things and ask God to act.
3. Revelation: The Holy Spirit might nudge your heart or bring an idea to mind for a particular need or area of prayer. Listen and pray!
4. Scripture: You might have read part of God's Word in preparation for your walk. Perhaps the Holy Spirit might bring a Scripture to mind. Pray about that passage and how it might impact the people in that area.

Here are five areas of influence that you can focus on during your prayer walk:

1. Government: Look for and pray over government centers such as courthouses, commission buildings, or law enforcement offices. Pray for the area's protection, for justice, and for godly wisdom for its leaders.
2. Business and commerce: Look for and pray over commercial centers such as financial districts or shopping areas. Pray for righteous investments and good stewardship of resources. Pray for economic justice and opportunity and for generous and godly givers who put people before profits.
3. Education: Look for and pray over educational centers such as schools and administration buildings, vocational training centers, community colleges, and universities. Pray for righteous educators to teach God's truth and protect the minds of their students. Pray that God will intervene when necessary to

prevent the spread of lies or confusion. Pray that these places would send out wise citizens who have hearts to serve and lead.

4. Communication: Look for and pray over communication centers such as radio stations, TV stations, and newspaper publishers. Pray for God's Story and the testimony of His followers to be spread throughout the city and around the world. Pray that His message is delivered through His medium to His multitudes and that God's people everywhere will see God's work.

5. Spirituality: Look for and pray over spiritual centers such as church buildings, mosques, or temples. Pray that every spiritual seeker would find peace and comfort in Jesus and not be distracted or confused by any false religion.

As you walk and pray, be alert for opportunities and listen for promptings by God's Spirit to pray for individuals and groups you meet along the way. You can say, "We're praying for this community. Is there anything in particular we can pray for you about?" Or say, "I'm praying for this area. Do you know anything in particular we should pray for?" After listening to their response, you can ask about their own needs. If they share, pray for them right away. If the Lord leads, you may pray about other needs as well. Use the word BLESS to help you remember five different ways you can pray:

1. Body (health)
2. Labor (job and finances)
3. Emotional (morale)
4. Social (relationships)
5. Spiritual

In most cases, people are grateful you care enough to pray. If the person is not a Christian, your prayer may open the door to a spiritual conversation and an opportunity to share your story and God's story. You can invite them to be a part of a Bible study or even host one in their home. If the person is a Christian, you can invite him to join your prayer walk or train him how he can prayer walk and use simple steps like praying for areas of influence or the BLESS prayer to grow God's family even more (ZumeProject, Session 1).

Self-Feeding in Body Life

God uses His body of believers, the Church, to grow us spiritually. As the gathering of believers, we are connected. His Word says that, in Jesus, we are many parts of one body, and we all belong to each other. In other words, we're not just connected to God, we're also connected with each other. He says to submit to one another. He also says to serve one another. Each of us has different strengths, and each has weaknesses. He expects us to use our strengths to help others who may be weak. He expects us to allow others to help us in our weakness using the strengths He has given them. The Bible says He has given each follower some special abilities. Be sure to use them to help each other, passing on to others the many kinds of blessings He grants us.

Boldness in the Face of a Passive World

When it comes to our faith, historically, many of us have lived in a somewhat passive world. Many of us have never had to take a stand for our faith, much less be persecuted for it in any way. Besides attending church, how does our faith normally play out? For some of us, the answer would have to be, not very boldly.

Photo 21: Our goal is to become like Jesus, then multiply.

By contrast, CPM/DMM approaches change all that. CPM/DMM trainers ask us constantly to filter all our exchanges, looking for people who might be seeking God. We are constantly trying to obey what we've learned, then train others to do the same. When given the opportunity, we are more overt about sharing our testimonies and the story of God redeeming the lost. Our goal is to become like Jesus, then multiply. These are all very intentional, ACTIVE steps. We have to learn to be bold and active in the face of a passive, reactive world.

Reproducibility

Because we are constantly seeking to multiply, we have to figure out how to do everything in reproducible ways. For example, if we meet with others to train them on prayer or accountability, we should avoid meeting in restaurants and buying their meals/coffees every time. Why? Because our goal is not only to train others, but to model the **process** of training others. What if some of our group members feel they can't afford buying meals or refreshments every time? If that's the case, we can't possibly stage our three-thirds group in a rented facility. Everything we do has to be reproducible. We design the entire system to multiply from the beginning.

Embracing the Vision

We can talk about all the tools, all the habits, and all the principles – but there is one other key factor (perhaps second only to prayer in fostering the initiation of Kingdom movements) that we simply dare not overlook. For a movement to happen, someone or some group has to embrace it and engage the group with passion. Someone typically needs to ask the question, "What's it going to take for all the people in _____ (this city, people group, or region, or country) to hear about and follow Jesus?" That question – "What's it going to take..." - is so different from the question that so many people ask. Many (most?) ask, "Lord, what can I do?" When an advocate rises up embracing a vision for reaching the whole group, suddenly the questions are reframed. Instead of thinking about one individual at a time, or one church per year, for example, the question instead becomes, "How can I reach this group in my lifetime?"

How does this play out? For example, in traditional one-church-per-year mission work, we used to ask the question, "How can we launch one new church this year?" Asking that question prompts us to think in terms of winning 100 people. Furthermore, it assumes a template consisting of something like a) a building, b) a budget, c) a staff (the right staff), and d) programs. If we manage to end the year with a (single) new congregation of 75 people, we rejoice.

In the CPM/DMM paradigm, we can't afford to think in terms of one church. We have to dream of more rapid multiplication while at the same time dreaming of deeper roots for prayer, Bible reading, and multiplication.

This entire discussion became bigger than life for me when I recently interviewed a virtual pioneer in relaunching CPM/DMM approaches, Bill Smith. Bill would say, of course, that these are simple biblical methods that should never have been ignored in the first place; but the truth is, his humble yet firm commitment to these and other truths have helped launch them again on multiple fronts (maybe on multiple continents?) over the past 30 years. As I mentioned, Bill is a humble man, but he is unswervingly committed to the process of mentoring and coaching new disciple makers. He would be embarrassed if I mentioned the list of people into whose life he has spoken about these topics. But I will mention just two. He mentored Curtis Sergeant while Curtis was attending seminary. (Curtis wrote the Introduction and the Epilogue for this book). Bill also helped David Garrison (who wrote the Foreword) formulate the 10 universals for the first draft of his book about church-planting movements. Interestingly, Bill grilled me for the longest time ever about why I would invest time in writing this book. "If you really want to start a movement – if you really want to make a difference – don't write a book. Find a piece of the world to adopt and claim it for God. Then don't write anyone else until you've asked and answered the critical question, "What's it going to take to win this city?" In Bill's framework for life, why would we want to answer email? Why would we write an article? Why would we spend time doing any administration? Invest in people. Tell God's story. Share your testimony. Keep looking for someone who will help you, then multiply your lives into others.

In fact, Bill is so brutally honest that he even went so far as to point out that, "It's not about a strategy, really. You can't reduce it to a methodology. You can't prescribe it even." I finally asked, "Well, then, what, pray tell, is **IT**?" Honestly, he had to ponder for a second. But he finally said, "**IT** rests in the heart, hands, and feet of a committed Ying Kai for a Chinese group or an unstoppable David Watson for a group in India." Then he went to meddling with pretty much everything I thought I had understood to be sacred. "The truth is, I served on the verification team for Ying Kai's movement. And yes, my team went to the 17th generation, and I have all the reports to prove it. But in spite of everything we say about Ying Kai and that movement in China, it wasn't really about any particular prescribed strategy." I begged to know, "Well, then - what **WAS** it?" His answer was surprising. "I think it was because Ying Kai had done a great job passing on a passion for finishing the task in that region. Ying designed his questions from an old Billy Graham tract. He didn't have the benefit of books like you're writing. What he DID have was commitment. Disciple-makers who want to be true multipliers need that undying, unceasing, ruthlessly relentless passion that goes beyond any typical calling. And the passion has to be for the whole people group - not just for one person." Bill happened to be involved in supervising David Watson's work in India, too. (This guy. Can you imagine the stories he has?) "Next time you get David Watson in a room, ask him for the details of what he did to launch that million-person movement to Christ in India. You'll be shocked. The method looks very official now in a book or on paper, but I've got the monthly reports for the entire saga. A big piece of this boiled down to David Watsons's undying belief that these people were headed to a Christless eternity unless something or someone intervened in their lives. Pass **THAT** on to the people you're mentoring and training and you've got the makings of a movement."

This intangible energy – the kind of energy that causes a person to lay down his life for a city – that's the energy we need to recover from the apostles in the book of Acts. They didn't have a 3 circles presentation; but they believed that unless they intervened, entire cities

Photo 22: We have to eat, breathe, and unceasingly pray for our city's salvation and for everyone in it.

were headed to eternal punishment. Bill Smith's point sounds accurate to me: Unless or until today's church begins acting and behaving like this is the most important work in the world, the majority of our planet's seven billion inhabitants will never embrace Jesus as their Lord. We have to **believe** in a real Hell. We have to **passionately** want to snatch them from darkness. It has to become **personal** for us. We have to eat, breathe, and unceasingly **pray** for our city's salvation and for everyone in it. If we can raise up a new generation of witnesses with that kind of long-term commitment, we **can** see multiplying movements, multiplying leaders, and multiplying churches in our land – and in **every** land.

But you have to want it - for Christ's sake. Do you? Will you? Your answer will determine whether or not this book was worth writing.

Questions for Discussion:

1. Compare and contrast the "SOAPS" Bible study approach to the one you're using now. What are the advantages or disadvantages of each?

2. Do you believe that being in an accountability group (such as the one described in this chapter) would be helpful for the typical believer? Do you think the typical believer is in such a group? If not, can you venture some guesses as to why or why not?

3. What would concern you most about participating in a 3/3 group, as described in this chapter? Explain what you think might be some benefits and also some risks.

4. This chapter offered two key approaches for increasing our own involvement in prayer. (Can you remember them both?) How do these approaches compare or contrast with typical prayer approaches used in churches you've attended? Give examples.

5. Consider the town, city, people group, or country where your church is located or where you hope to make disciples. How does it change the way you think to ask the question, "What's it going to take for all these people to hear the Good News and follow Jesus?"

CHAPTER 10

IMPACTS ON DISCIPLE-MAKING

We've discussed the role of the Holy Spirit. When it's all said and done, God is the one who causes a CPM/DMM to take place. But as we've mentioned, some of our own actions can accelerate or impede a movement from taking place. Movements are also impacted by the surrounding environment. In addition, the context itself can also impact the formation of a movement.

Persecution

God works through the persecution, suffering, sacrifice and loss that we endure on behalf of Jesus. Not only does it increase our resolve and improve our resilience, but, in addition, it actually grows us spiritually. When people oppress and hurt us because we love and obey Jesus, or when bad things happen as a result of our faith, God uses those persecutions and sufferings to develop and refine our character and make us more like Jesus. He strengthens and purifies our faith, equips us for ministry, and allows us to serve others who are suffering in a special way, all while making Himself known more clearly to everyone who watches us and knows our pain. God tells us that, as followers of Jesus, we should expect to be persecuted. Jesus said,

> Blessed are you when people insult you, persecute you and falsely say all kinds of evil against you because of me. Rejoice and be glad,

because great is your reward in heaven, for in the same way they persecuted the prophets who were before you (Matthew 5:11-12).

Simple tools like 3/3 groups and accountability groups give followers of Jesus an opportunity to share the persecutions and sufferings they experience. These groups give you a chance to teach disciples that God's Word says we should expect hard times and to equip them in how to respond well by trusting God's love even when things go wrong.

Due to the above reasoning (and other factors that we don't yet totally understand), though it seems counter-intuitive, CPMs/DMMs seem to occur more often in environments in which Christians are being persecuted for their faith. In environments of persecution (even extreme persecution), only the most courageous believers remain. So when the world looks at the church, they are astonished. And in a strange way, even though onlookers are fearful of repression and persecution, they are even drawn and attracted.

This happened in the early Church.

And they devoted themselves to the apostles's teaching, to the fellowship, to the breaking of bread, and to the prayers. Then fear came over everyone, and many wonders and signs were being performed through the apostles. Now all the believers were together and held all things in common. They sold their possessions and property and distributed the proceeds to all, as anyone had a need. Every day they devoted themselves to meeting together in the temple complex, and broke bread from house to house. They ate their food with a joyful and humble attitude, praising God and having favor with all the people. And every day the Lord added to them those who were being saved (Acts 2:42-48).

All of this growth was taking place in the midst of severe persecution. But think about it — in those trials, believers become stronger and newcomers are inspired. The blood of martyrs is the seed of church-planting and disciple-making movements.

It continued in Acts 5:18 when religious leaders arrested Jesus's closest followers and had them put into prison. In verse 19, an angel opens the door of the jail and brings them out, instructing them to go tell God's story and their testimonies to the people — in public! In verse 21, they do as they were instructed, so the religious leaders haul them in again for questioning (verse 27). The leaders beat them (verse 40), then release them, and what do Jesus's followers do? They rejoice because they had been counted worthy of suffering for His name (verse 41). So what do they do after that? They continue telling other people about Jesus (verse 42). So what happens to the church? It begins increasing **rapidly**. It's that rapid growth we crave again today. And it seems to happen all the more rapidly during persecution.

Time

Time (believers's availability and/or accessibility) favors CPMs/DMMs. If church members are stuck behind cubicle walls for 60-70 hours a week, they have fewer opportunities to share their stories. By contrast, if they work a job that allows them to travel and speak with people regularly, then their job itself — their own time — helps them multiply.

Of course, the ultimate deadline for the end of all CPMs/DMMs is the end of time itself. In order to launch movements, we hope and pray that God will delay His second coming. Of course, maybe He's delaying it BECAUSE He knows we need more time. Matthew writes, "This good news of the kingdom will be proclaimed in all the world as a testimony to all nations. And then the end will come" (Matthew 24:14). Peter adds, "The Lord does not delay His promise, as some understand delay, but is patient with you, not wanting any to perish but all to come to re-pentance" (2 Peter 3:9). So, maybe all this time, God has been granting us just a bit more time so that all creation can hear. For a CPM/DMM to happen, we need time.

Of course, the converse should be true. We can never assume how much time we really do have. As a result, we need to multiply as rapidly and as widely as possible.

Cultural Understanding

Cross-cultural communication can be daunting. We understand and hear the language differences. We might have to work on them daily for a year or more, but at least we're aware. One of the problems with cross-cultural differences is that, because we're usually looking at the other culture through the grid of our home culture, we are sometimes (often?) unaware of cross-cultural differences. Even the differences we can detect might seem quaint or even interesting at first; but after some amount of time, those same differences might begin to annoy or frustrate us. If we're trying to make disciples cross-culturally, it's super-important for us to appreciate the differences.

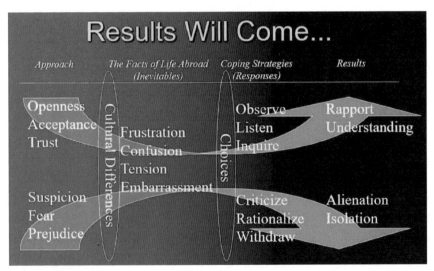

Figure 23. The Impact that Our Entry Posture Can Have on Cross-Cultural Differences.

This model (see Figure 23. The Impact that Our Entry Posture Can Have on Cross-Cultural Differences.) might help us comprehend the impact that our entry posture can have on cross-cultural differences.

This model teaches that, when we enter another culture, we inevitably experience cross-cultural differences which engender a certain amount of frustration, confusion, tension, and embarrassment. These inevitable facts of life force us to make a choice. According to the model, we can either choose to observe, listen, and inquire — or we can criticize, rationalize, and withdraw. Using this model, Ted Ward taught that, if we approach a new culture with openness, acceptance, and trust, we were much more likely to transition through the cross-cultural stress along the "upper track," and, by doing so, our observations and inquiries would help us develop rapport and understanding.

However, if we entered a new culture feeling a ton of suspicion, fear, and prejudice, our critical spirit and our rationalizations would end up prompting us to withdraw, which would result in alienation and isolation from the people.

It would seem, then, that the environment in which we find ourselves and, especially, our response to it, can impact not only our ability to form healthy relationships, but also our functional ability to articulate truth in a healthy and effective way. The better we adapt, the more likely it is that we can share our story and God's story with the people to whom we've been sent.

Common Language/Culture

Another environmental factor that can impact the formation of a CPM/DMM is having a common language. We see this in the New Testament. Rome was in a conquering mood. In fact, they had taken over most of the territory from Jerusalem all the way over to the Atlantic Ocean. Koine Greek had become the common language of the Eastern Mediterranean so Rome embraced it as one of the two common languages of their entire empire (Millar, 2006, p. 279). Because of this common language, the church could spread quite rapidly across countless islands and villages of the known world (Treadgold, 1997, p. 5).

In today's world, the church still flows naturally along language and cultural lines. Once it hits a barrier of understanding or acceptance, the growth of the church often slows or stops cold. For this reason, missiologists have classified the world into "people groups," largely categorized by ethnic background and cultural similarity. CPMs/DMMs flow quite naturally until they butt up against barriers — like the edge of a cultural or language grouping. Joshua Project, which can be found at http://www.joshuaproject.net, keeps careful records of these data. They describe these people groups as being reached, unreached, and even unengaged.

- **Reached**: Two percent or more of the group identify themselves as being evangelical believers and/or they live in an area in which 5% or more of the people identify themselves as Christians in general (even if they are actually only nominally so).
- **Unreached**: Fewer than 2% claim to be evangelical believers; fewer than 5% consider themselves Christians (even on a nominal or national sense).
- **Unengaged**: Researchers use this term to describe a group with little or no engagement by those who would proclaim Christ as Lord. (Some groups, like Finishing the Task, use a simple benchmark such as "fewer than 1 gospel witness per 50,000 inhabitants.")

So within one group with a common language and/or culture, we assume that one strategy, if it's effective in general, would be effective throughout the group. Conversely, a CPM/DMM would have a hard time catching on throughout an entire group if the strategy is ineffective from the beginning. For example, in a tribe that lives on the coast, maybe we propose organizing groups around lunchtime discussions at cooperative fish markets - because those are natural gathering places for men coming back from morning fishing runs. But 25 kilometers inland, we end up finding more fruit by organizing groups around campfires after dark because only then do the men come back from their fields. We're flexible in our strategy because we see that life is different among the unique people groups and tribes we're trying to reach.

Obviously, there are exceptions to this norm. Similar strategies sometimes "jump" from one people group to another, even when those groups speak different languages. Unfortunately, we can't always **assume** that this will be the case. Thus, we always have to enter a new context with "people group eyes," prepared for the worst (dreaming up differing strategies for differing groups, even if they're neighboring) but hoping for the best (seeing a tribe reach the tribe next door without having to force the issue at all – in complete unity and harmony).

Persons of Peace

A Person of Peace can help rapidly reproduce disciple-making even in a place where followers of Jesus are few and far between. When Jesus sent out His disciples to a new territory to make disciples, He gave them a simple but strategic command.

> Do not take a purse or bag or sandals; and do not greet anyone on the road. When you enter a house, first say, 'Peace to this house.' If someone who promotes peace is there, your peace will rest on them; if not, it will return to you. Stay there, eating and drinking whatever they give you, for the worker deserves his wages. Do not move around from house to house (Luke 10:4-7).

What does all that mean? When we think of making disciples, our first thought might be — We better get our finances in order, pick an obvious target, and have a clear plan of action. If Jesus said go, we had better go and keep on going! We should tell everyone, everywhere, all the time! But Jesus, in His instructions, seemed a lot less worried about finances and fervor and a lot more concerned about focus. Jesus wanted His disciples looking for and investing in a Person of Peace. When you want to make disciples in a place where few or none exist, then looking for a Person of Peace might be the most important thing you do.

A Person of Peace is someone who:

- **Is open** to hearing Your Story, God's Story, and the Good News of Jesus.
- **Is hospitable** and **welcomes** you into his home or his workplace or to join events with family and friends.
- **Knows others** (or is **known by others**) and who is excited to draw together a small group or even a crowd.
- Is **faithful** and **shares** what he learns with others - even after you're gone.

In the Bible, we learn of Jesus and His followers encountering the most unlikely Persons of Peace ever. In the region of the Gadarenes, Jesus met a demon-possessed man who lived isolated and in chains (Mark 5). We would never think of him as a Person of Peace, but he was **open** to hear from Jesus. He was **hospitable** and **welcomed** Jesus to where he lived. He was **well known** and could easily draw a crowd - even if only for his outrageous behavior. And Jesus found that he was **faithful** and **shared** what Jesus meant to him with his family, his community, and his whole country. In fact, when Jesus came back to that area, a great crowd gathered, excited to see the man about whom they had heard so much. In Samaria, Jesus met a woman at a well (John 4). She was **open** to Jesus, willing to be **hospitable**, and answer His request for a drink. We learn she had five husbands and was living with still another man. In a small town, she was sure to be **known by others**. After Jesus spoke to her, she was **faithful** and **shared** so much and so quickly that the entire town asked Jesus to stay and share with them, too. And He did. So, if a Person of Peace can live almost anywhere, do almost anything, and be almost anyone we know or meet - how do we find one?

Here are three simple ways:

1. We **ask** for recommendations from people in the community - Who's someone that's trusted here? Is there someone in this place who thinks of others before themselves? If we hear the same name again and again then we try to meet them, share spiritual ideas, and see if they're open to hear and share.
2. We **offer** to pray for someone while prayer walking, or at work, or at the game - wherever there's an opportunity - and then turn that prayer into a spiritual conversation.
3. We **introduce** spiritual ideas into every conversation to see if God is working in a person's life. If they are open and willing, then we ask if they would be willing to gather a group to discuss even more.

Ask for recommendations, **offer** to pray, and **introduce** spiritual ideas. These are all ways we can begin the process of finding a Person of Peace. No matter how we find them, remember Jesus said a Person of Peace is someone with whom we should be spending most of our disciple-making time. It's easy to think that the most "fair" use of our time is to give away a little bit of ourselves to everyone, equally. Jesus said, and showed, that He doesn't want us to be shallow with everyone but to give deeply to a few. Jesus often attracted crowds, but the Bible tells us again and again that Jesus would draw away from those crowds to spend most of His time with just twelve of His closest followers. There were a number of times when Jesus would invest even more time with a smaller group of just three. Think about it. Jesus had much more power, energy, authority, discipline, wisdom, knowledge, understanding, and compassion than we have. If He chose to spend His time investing deeply in just a few and told His own disciples to do the same, doesn't it make sense then that we should follow and share His perfect pattern? Persons of Peace: they're difficult to find, but when you finally encounter them, they're worth their weight in gold.

Photo 24: Persons of peace can introduce us to new social networks.

Questions for Discussion:

1. Offer some of your best guesses as to why you believe the church seems to flourish in the midst of persecution.

2. Examine your own life and the amount of time you have to add activities or approaches. When you read the ideas in this book and process the time it would take to implement them, is it sobering for you? Why or why not? How will you personally decide about your time priorities?

3. Have you ever experienced cross-cultural confusion or "shock?" Give an example.

4. The author wrote in this chapter that the church can expand rapidly within a common language and/or culture. Is there a language or cultural group that you wish could know and follow Jesus? If so, describe it.

5. This chapter presents the concept of filtering for a "person of peace" to help introduce you to another culture. Have you ever experienced anything like this (someone introducing you to a new group or crowd)? If so, describe how it worked. Analyze how it might work with the Good News of Jesus.

CHAPTER 11

TEMPLATES FOR TRAINING

If there's one thing everyone agrees upon, it's the importance of prayer as a first step. But after that, the sky is the limit. In fact, throughout the world, one can often hear a quote that goes something like this: "The truth is — nobody knows exactly how to do these movements". We know something about the practices that prevent them. We can recognize some universal practices or common elements in all or most of them. But there's no magic formula. We can't say, "Do this and a movement will result." It just doesn't happen that way. As a result, we can only introduce proposed templates and theories for jump-starting the process. The rest will always be a work of the Spirit.

What we can tell you is that a movement, when it does happen, makes everything else appear sluggish. Once multiplication kicks in, you'll know it. Like in the book of Acts, there will be so many people coming to Christ, it will have gotten the attention of everyone around you. It will have turned the world right-side-up.

So in this chapter, we introduce proposed training templates for testing and evaluation. As we gather information, data, and experience, we hope to improve this chapter — and this entire book. May God train us all in the way that He wants His Kingdom to grow. For now, though, in view of everything we've covered so far, here are some ways one might try to jump-start the process in your neighborhood, church, and/or nation.

The Organic Way

CPM/DMM trainers have a watchword: "Start small to grow big. Start slow to go fast." It might sound a bit like an oxymoron. However, it has proven true time and time again. If we try to over-program CPM/DMM practices, they become just that: programs. Unfortunately, programs can have a fairly short lifespan. People get tired of programs. They wear out. CPM/DMM practices need to be life. They need to be perpetual. They need to be natural. No one has to tell you to breathe. If you stop breathing, you die. CPM/DMM practices have to become like breathing. If we want church growth to be the norm, then we would be a lot better off if these practices would also become the norm in each of our lives. If we want stale or dead churches, all we have to do is make CPM/DMM another program. Wow. Please Lord, prevent us from doing that.

But there's another reason to start small. We need genuine people. We need people who have normalized CPM/DMM life practices from the inside out. If we introduce CPM/DMM as a program or "just another choice from the church menu," people begin to perceive it as something akin to attending the church social or the volleyball outing. "It was fun for a while. We met some new people. But next season, I think I'll play soccer instead." CPM/DMM practices can't become surface level. They have to become heart-level. They have to grow deeply. In the past, that's been tough to do with 200 listeners in the audience. Movements seem to happen best in the context of small groups which reproduce. Remember, they're not just **any** kind of small group. They are a small group of **obedient** practitioners — people who obey, train, and share with others what they're learning. They are, in a word, **intentional** about their faith. It's tough to train that in a group of 200.

Now please don't misunderstand. It can be trained in a relatively short order. Within 4 weeks (in the context of an obedience-based discovery Bible study program and given the right order) one can pick up these habits and start making a difference. Beware of any method that introduces these practices in large groups or even moderate-sized ones.

In fact, if the group is larger than a dozen or so people, real change ... real heart-felt obedience that leads to normalization... is rare, at best.

For this reason, experience has shown that the beginnings of a new movement won't look all that promising. If you're accustomed to big launches, you probably want fireworks, loud music, and fog machines. You probably want hundreds of people. As a result, it will look like the church is off to a great start. You might even experience additions. Additions give you steady growth, at least in the early-going. Add a person every cycle and — bam... in 10 cycles, you've added 10 people. Solid growth, right? It looks like this:

Table 2: Growth by Addition

$$1+1=2$$
$$2+1=3$$
$$3+1=4$$
$$4+1=5$$
$$5+1=6$$
$$6+1=7$$
$$7+1=8$$
$$8+1=9$$
$$9+1=10$$

And we're thrilled with 10 people. Rightfully so. At least it's progress in the right direction, right? The trouble is, we'll never keep up with population growth if we just focus on additions. Populations are growing faster than that. To keep up with population growth, we need to look at a multiplicative growth. Multiplicative growth (CPM/DMM-type growth) looks different. During a rather humble start-up phase, it looks like you're focusing on rather small numbers. There's no big 1000-person start-up. There are no fireworks, no loud music, and, unfortunately, there's no fog. Even if/when this group multiplies, it would likely just double or triple. There are still likely just two or three groups. So the entire attendance, added together, might be just a dozen people, even after a full cycle (however long a cycle is). So it looks rather slow at first. The difference is, these groups grow geometrically, not arithmetically.

The lines above represent 10 "cycles," with each cycle adding one person. In the chart below, we grow in a geometric progression (which is way faster than an arithmetic progression). We start with one person, facilitating a group of six people. Following the first cycle, the one group multiplies into three groups. If each of those three groups also has six participants, there are now 18 people in all. At the end of 10 weeks, each of the six groups multiplies by three again — which means now we have nine. Ten weeks later, those nine become 27. Multiplicative growth doesn't result in just 10 people after 10 cycles. It ends up with over 118,000. So the early growth looks slow and even small. However, multiplication yields huge results as exponential growth takes hold later. (After 21 cycles, if those results were to hold steady, the whole world is participating in groups.) Take a look at the accompanying table to see the results.

Photo 25: Explaining the miracle of geometric growth is about like trying to explain the way snowflakes are made up of water molecules. It's difficult to explain – until you see the magic.

So, don't hesitate to start small to grow big. Train as you go, and ask people to train others as they go, too. The results, in the end, will startle. Make sure you are thorough with each lesson's expectation. Multiplication only happens if everyone understands his or her part. What does this mean for you if you want to launch a movement? Maybe the best way to launch a new movement is to recruit five other people and form a six-person group. Then follow the chart above. Make sure you invest heavily in those five people for an entire training cycle. Then help each pair in your group (your "pair" included) to start a new group of its own. Repeat the entire process. Don't forget to coach your pairs to multiply. Dare them to greatness. Stick with them through multiplication, and then train your pairs to coach **THEIR** pairs to multiply too. You can do this without fireworks. You won't need loud music; you certainly don't need fog. Just do the simple tools talked about in this book.

Table 3: Growth by multiplication (geometric growth).

generation	# of groups	in each group	total # of people involved
1	1	6	6
2	3	6	18
3	9	6	54
4	27	6	162
5	81	6	486
6	243	6	1458
7	729	6	4374
8	2187	6	13122
9	6561	6	39366
10	19683	6	118098
11	59049	6	354294
12	177147	6	1062882
13	531441	6	3188646
14	1594323	6	9565938
15	4782969	6	28697814
16	14348907	6	86093442
17	43046721	6	258280326
18	129140163	6	774840978
19	387420489	6	2324522934
20	1162261467	6	6973568802

Drop. Dead. Simple.

You won't need to stage big group get-togethers. No need to rent a theater. Just train and multiply. That's it.

We might call this method the "organic" or "natural" way. Maybe this is the way Jesus intended it. No buildings, no paid staff, no programs, no budgets, and, like we said before, no fog.

Nay-sayers will tell you the steam will run out. Remember, Ying Kai used exactly this approach to forge a movement of two million people. Simple. Easy. Just train trainers.

In fact, you might ask, why would we consider doing anything else? Good question. The only answer we can think of is — for some reason, the chains break down. Some groups inevitably break up. Some don't even totally form. Some die out. People are busy. Sometimes they get distracted; but hey — it's been like that since the time of Jesus. Remember the parable of the four soils (Matthew 13:1-23, Mark 4:1-20, and Luke 8:4-15)? Maybe your job isn't to look for lots and lots of group members. Maybe your job is to look for "fourth-soil people." These fourth-soil people are the ones in whom it is worthwhile to invest a lot of your time because they're the ones who will multiply and produce fruit 40-, 60- and 100-fold.

In summary, the above method isn't really very complicated at all. Does it help to have tools and a structure for following Jesus? Without a doubt, it's easier to follow a path when the trail is blazed in front of us. However, even those patterns are rather simple. The more complex the pattern, the more likely it is that people will get bogged down in trying to multiply. Complexity has a way of doing that. Also, the pattern needs to be easily replicated by people with regular jobs. We can't afford to wait for enough paid staff to win the world. (If that were the case, they would have already done it.) We need to figure out how to win the world with lay people. So even if you're planning to implement this "organic" or "natural" method of launching groups, you will still need some kind of guide. You could try, for example, Nathan and Kari Shank's book, *Four Fields of Kingdom Growth* (Shank & Shank). (You could also try using the very book you're reading now!)

Decades ago, George Patterson wrote a set of booklets for use in his own work in Honduras. Those books are still available via the web at sites like this one: http://www.paul-timothy.net. Using these little booklets, Dr. Patterson launched a movement of churches that still stands as a great pattern for all of us, decades later. (Reminder: You can listen to an interview with Dr. Patterson about this movement (and more) at http://www.moredisciples.com/webinars.)

These days, however, there is perhaps a simpler tool — and it's one that won't require you to order a book, or a DVD, or pay a subscription fee.

Zúme

Zúme is the Greek word for yeast. Jesus tells us that the Kingdom of God is like a woman who took a small amount of "zúme" and put it into a great amount of dough. As she worked the yeast into the mix, it spread until all of the dough was leavened (Matthew 13). Jesus was showing us that an ordinary person can take something very small and use it to

Figure 26: Zúme is a web-driven course for those wishing to learn how to make disciples who make disciples.

make an impact that's very big! The dream of Zúme (the web-facilitated training course) is to do what Jesus said — to help ordinary people around the world use small tools to make a big impact in God's Kingdom! Jesus's original instructions to His followers were simple.

Then Jesus came to them and said, "All authority in heaven and on earth has been given to me. Therefore go and make disciples of all nations, baptizing them in the name of the Father and of the Son and of the Holy Spirit, and teaching them to obey everything I have commanded you. And surely I am with you always, to the very end of the age" (Matthew 28:18-20).

Jesus's command was simple — make disciples. His instructions on how to do that were simple — make disciples wherever you're going.

Make disciples by baptizing them in the name of the Father, Son, and Holy Spirit. Make disciples by teaching them to obey all He commanded. So, what are the steps to make a disciple?

1. We make disciples all the time - wherever we're going and as we go.
2. When someone decides to follow Jesus, they should be baptized.
3. As they grow, we should teach every disciple how to obey everything that Jesus commanded.

Since one of the things He commanded is to make disciples, that means that every disciple who follows Jesus needs to learn how to make disciples, too. Those disciples are to make disciples. Furthermore, those disciples are to make disciples, too. Zúme works if and when everyone realizes that everyone needs to be involved in multiplying disciples (ZumeProject, Session 1).

Zúme consists of 10 sessions. Each session lasts roughly two hours each, depending on the length of discussion and size of the group. Zúme uses video and audio to help your group understand basic principles of multiplying disciples. The course utilizes group discussions to help your group think through what's being shared, along with simple exercises to help your group put what you're learning into practice. There are always session challenges (like homework) to help your group keep learning and growing between sessions. (Note: The 10th session is somewhat advanced. During the first 12-18 months of implementation, several of us skipped session 10 with first-time participants. However, the Zúme development team finally pointed out to us that, unless we picked up session 10 during the participants' first training, he or she might never actually go back and watch it afterward. As a result, we've begun implementing Zúme as a full 10-week course rather than 9 weeks alone.)

You can start a Zúme group anytime and anywhere. If you are the facilitator, you can make sure you start talking about the importance of multiplication from the very start. You can let your group know about the miracle of exponential (geometric) growth, as compared with arithmetic growth. In every session, all along the way, we ask the facilitator to sprinkle in seeds of thought about multiplication of two key vehicles: new Zúme groups (for outreach) and new 3/3 groups (new spiritual families). Another way to address it might be to ask, "How do we help each participant in the group become great at loving God, loving others, and making disciples?" Loving God and loving others will compel us all to make sure we're starting new 3/3 groups and participating in one as our spiritual family. Making disciples might also include multiplying Zúme groups as well because Zúme is a great tool to help a person understand how to become, make, and multiply disciples. Therefore, the concept of "members of two groups" is key. We need that regular

spiritual family, and we need Zúme to help us expand the Kingdom to places and people where it isn't. So, in every Zúme group, we suggest that you look into each person's life and dare them to become a disciple worth multiplying by doing both — launching a Zúme group (or helping others do so) and participating in a 3/3 group as one's spiritual family.

Photo 27: Zúme groups try to help each participant become great at loving God, loving others and making disciples.

As mentioned above, Zúme can be used as "the template" in a natural or organic approach. Let's consider that approach first.

Start Zúme informally, behind the scenes

This approach is perhaps the easiest to implement. Rather than recruiting "permission" from church leaders or other team members, you just begin implementing Zúme informally by pulling together a group of your own.

Advantages:

- You don't need anyone's permission. You can start today or tomorrow or whenever you choose.
- You can facilitate the group however you wish — i.e., choose the night of the week in the location and at the time you prefer.
- You can personally make sure the group starts well (with everything you're learning in this book).
- You can implement the group in the context of a local church (your own or another), or you can alternatively choose to implement the group apart from any existing church structure, hoping that maybe the Zúme groups themselves **become** church for the participants.

Disadvantages:

- Because you aren't working within the context of a larger community (an existing church or agency), some prospective group members might be concerned about doctrine or identity of the group. This is, of course, a needless concern because you will be following the principles in this book (and Zúme itself), which exalt the Bible as the highest authority. Still, there might exist someone who will wonder, "Whose doctrine are you going to follow?" because the group isn't affiliated with an existing church body which they can categorize.
- You won't have a building (e.g., a church building) for your meeting. Of course, this is a needless concern, too, because every trainer is quick to point out the CPM/DMM groups quickly outgrow their buildings anyway.
- Because you're not under the "shelter" of a larger infrastructure, it will feel as if you have to answer questions and problems on your own. This is a needless concern as well because you'll have this book — and Zúme coaches, if you desire. (Every screen in

Zúme contains a link at the bottom to ask for help. There are volunteers ready to help you at every level, including county and state coordinators.)

- This approach will feel small... and maybe even weak. It's not. Start small to grow big; start slow to go fast.

In addition to doing Zúme "naturally" or "organically," you can also utilize Zúme in conjunction with your local church. Let's look at that approach next.

Ask your church (or some other church) if you could start Zúme within their infrastructure.

This approach is only one tiny increment more complicated.

Advantages:

- With this model, you have a covering. If this is your home church, you presumably like their doctrine — and so will those you're trying to reach, presumably. They won't think you're a "cult."
- You might be able to use the building, if that's what you want. Maybe some people will be wary of hosting people in their homes. If there's space at the church, you won't have to worry about this concern.
- The church staff and leadership, if they're supportive of CPM/DMM principles and life practices, will likely appreciate Zúme very much. It's free, and there's no DVD to order, no satellite broadcast payment to cough up, and no book to buy. (The *Zúme Resource Guidebook*, available through a link in the first session, is free to download and print on your own printer.) The staff and leadership might appreciate your concerns and questions. They could be informed and helpful. They might answer every question.
- This approach will feel more official and appropriate, since you're working within the leadership of a local church.

Disadvantages:

- Some local churches may not be able to support a CPM/DMM or Zúme approach for various reasons. For example, they may require small groups to use the church's curriculum, or may need approval from the church's denominational headquarters for outside curriculum. There's just no predicting without checking.
- Zúme might feel like too big of a risk for a lead pastor and his ministerial staff. In fact, a pastor could even feel like Zúme might threaten the authority of the church. If Zúme participants begin having their "simple church" needs met by the Zúme Group (or something it launches), the pastor may be concerned that people will start attending the Zúme group and skipping church. He might also wonder how offerings will be affected.

Photo 28: Asking a pastor to allow you to try Zúme in a new context doesn't have to be scary. But we do have to give it some thought.

- At the very least, leaders in the church might wonder how Zúme participants fit in with the larger small group picture. If the church is doing an "all-church study," someone on the staff or in the leadership might expect the Zúme groups to join the same study, which would require the Zúme group(s) to give up their approach (discovery-based learning using the seven questions) during the entire length of the all-church study.
- Some might hesitate to come to the Zúme group if they perceive that joining the Zúme group is tantamount to "leaving their church." If they DO join, they might fear that their church leaders will fear that their own doctrine might be compromised.

CPM/DMM strategies should not be perceived to compete with or replace local churches. For further information refer to the discussion under the heading: "How Does CPM/DMM View Existing Churches?" in Chapter 13.

Implementation: There are several different models you could try in implementing this approach.

Leader-First Approach

Ask the church to suggest existing Bible study group leaders (or recruit leaders within the church yourself), and seek to gather them for a meeting. Cast the vision for Zúme. Cover the "high points" of this book, for example — or ask someone else to come and do so out of his or her experience. This might be an implementer in a nearby town (maybe the person who told you about Zúme) or someone from a nearby church, agency, or college/university. After casting the vision, practice by actually doing the first session as a group of leaders. If there are 4-12 present (ideal), you can model being a facilitator for them. If there are more, break up the group into two Zúme groups and do the session independently; don't try to do the group with 25 people. It won't work. (This is not as ideal, because they won't get to see you modeling the session.) Cover basic 3/3 group facilitation concepts such as the following (see the training hand-out in the appendix):

- Stick to what's in the passage. Don't allow group members to bring up other passages or skip around through the Bible. If they try to do so, just gently interrupt, saying, "Carl, that's a great topic for after our three-thirds group session. Let's come back to that then. For now, let's stick to the passage. Brenda, what's another point that you thought about on this topic?"
- View Scripture as the highest authority. If someone tries to explain the meaning of a verse but you can't find that meaning in the passage, simply train them to ask the question, "Now where is that in this passage?"

- Keep conversation moving, but try to insure that everyone is participating equally. Make sure even non-Christians have a chance to interact, ask questions, and give insights — as long as they're taken directly from the passage. (Note: If your group happens to be 100% made up of Christians, you could consider relaxing this norm, as long as everyone in the group understands that with seekers and not-yet-believers, you would need to re-institute it.)
- Remember to move the group through the three-thirds format — looking back, looking up, and looking forward. Follow the simple instructions in the Zúme session (session six and following). Sessions 6-8 will train you on how to facilitate a group. Follow them well because they have shown to be effective in multiple contexts on multiple continents.
- After the demo 3/3 group ends, ask if there are questions and explain what will happen in the steps below.
- On a Sunday morning following the meeting (after you've introduced the course to leaders Saturday night), dedicate the entire sermon time to launching the Zúme/DMM strategy. (Visit www.MoreDisciples.com to download a sample sermon and slide presentation that you can customize for your own needs.) Your goals in this session are to:

  - Build a case for obedience-based disciple-making (see chapters 1-3).
  - Help listeners understand that the church worldwide isn't winning the population/attendance war. We might have maintained the same percentage in some cases (flat-line; stagnant), but population outside of Christ has been increasing for decades, both at home and around the world.
  - Use examples from this book to show case studies of movements that have, for example, brought more Muslims to Christ in the past 15 years than had come to Christ in the previous 15 centuries. Explain that you'd like to challenge the

church to understand and implement these same approaches in hopes that God might launch a movement in your midst.

- Stage a follow-up informational meeting for any who are interested in learning more. Treat it as a chance to field questions about the approach.
- Pass out cards to obtain names, phone numbers, and email addresses of those who attend. Near the end of the meeting, offer to add them to existing small group studies for the 10-week Zúme experience. If you have too many people to add them to existing groups, recruit new leaders and stage another training program later (resembling the Saturday night meeting). If God gives you a great deal of responses, contact an experienced implementer for help training new facilitators. Don't forget to give Him praise for what He is doing in your midst!
- Implement the 10-week study in concert with all the groups, if possible. Send out a couple of emails through the 10 weeks, thanking everyone for participating. Stay in touch with group leaders throughout the experience. Remind them to seek help if they need it, talk about multiplication a lot, preview what's going to happen in Session 9 — and cast a vision that at least three people out of each group would be led by God to start a new Zúme group (another generation). At the end of the 10 weeks, pull all participants together to field questions about the next "generation" of Zúme groups. Give help as needed but, at this point, coach the first generation group facilitators to challenge their respective group members to launch new groups. Pray for at least three groups to be birthed out of each existing Zúme group.

Start the second generation of groups together. Stay in touch with the original facilitators of the first generation groups. Ask them, in turn, to encourage and coach the new facilitators who agreed to start second generation groups. They are now implementing 2 Timothy 2:2.

- Pray that Zúme can continue to grow and involve members of your congregation; but whenever a group or generation adds new group members from outside your church, celebrate that (to the extent you can, without creating undue embarrassment for the newcomer). Zúme is designed for growth, not for maintenance.

Sunday-First Approach

The "Sunday-first" approach is just like the above "leaders-first" approach except for the sequencing. In the "Sunday-first" approach, you (or someone you recruit) launch with the Sunday morning meeting to the entire congregation, asking people to sign up for a follow-up training event (for example, at a luncheon following that very morning Sunday service, or on the upcoming Wednesday evening, or the subsequent Saturday morning) designed primarily to train facilitators of groups. Let the listeners know that, although it's primarily for facilitators, all are welcome to attend and participate, even if they're not sure whether or not they're feeling called to facilitate a group from the beginning.

- Stage the training and cover items similar to those mentioned above. (Also see the training hand-out in the Appendix of this book.)
- Emphasize that Zúme is designed to help disciples become a disciple worth multiplying, then to train us how actually to multiply.
- Emphasize from the very start that it would be a **great** outcome if a Zúme course spawns the creation of a 3/3 group (or several 3/3 groups). Another great outcome is if Zúme creates a team of mul-

Photo 29: Stay in touch with original facilitators of first generation groups.

tipliers who decide to stage another generation of Zúme groups. Starting a 3/3 group is like starting a "simple church." Multiplying Zúme groups is like multiplying leadership training courses.

- In a recent example of the Sunday-first approach, the church gave the entire Sunday worship service to the special initiative of introducing Zúme to the congregation of 650 believers in Louisville, Kentucky. I explained during the message that I'd be happy with three takers. In other words, I was up front about the fact that I would love to launch one (1) single Zúme group out of that Sunday morning. Instead, around 120 people signed up. We made simple sign-up forms with first name, last name, email, and phone. We also asked if they might be willing to serve as a facilitator **and** we asked if they spoke Spanish, since the Zúme course in Spanish is now completed. After the Sunday service, someone needed to type all the cards into a database. We used AgileCRM, but you could use whatever app or spreadsheet you desire. We staged a facilitator training night on the next Wednesday night. About 50 people were able to make it. Nearly 100% of those 50 people grouped together into seven Zúme groups that started the following week. Another three groups will start 10 weeks later along with the second generation Zúme groups or 3/3 groups. We've contacted them via the email address they provided and called them all at least once.
- It's preferable to train facilitators and let **them** 'recruit' their Zúme group. Trying to mix and match people who don't have a natural connection is a little bit awkward. What's more, by focusing on training facilitators, you will end up increasing your response because these new facilitators will know more people who would come if someone just invited them to take part.
- We have learned through these initial efforts that it will always be difficult to recruit an entire church full of people. Instead of focusing on getting **everyone** involved, just focus on engaging those who **want** to be involved. Just pray that the others will

either decide to jump on board in a later generation of multi-plication. At the end of the day, though, "you can lead a horse to water but you can't make him drink." In other words, if you try to give them a blessing and they won't receive it, then let the blessing return to you, shake the dust off your feet, and move on.

Live Trainings

Live trainings up the ante significantly. Compared to the approaches above (primarily Zúme), live trainings require that you:

- Find a time that everyone can attend "live."
- Engage a trainer with experience, presentation/training skills, and availability.
- Charge a registration fee (usually) to recover the cost of flying in the trainer(s).
- Intensify the training schedule (to reduce the number of days your trainer has to be at your location).
- Arrange for meals and/or other logistics that come from an extended-length program.

At the same time, many trainers believe that live trainings are more effective than any other approach because they are...

- The only approach which allows for direct oversight by a trainer who can give you direct input to improve your skill.
- The best option if you have questions or concerns.
- Totally interactive, making them more interesting than other options.

Unfortunately, there is no one clearinghouse for CPM/DMM trainers. As a result, finding one pretty much requires that you know someone. Some trainers are more experienced than others. Some have personal stories, resulting in lots more personal credibility. Others have become professional, itinerant trainers, meaning that they no longer have the time to work personally in the challenge of making and multiplying disciples, which might be a bit of a downer. Some are really articulate speakers, while others are less articulate but really great at making disciples. Bottom line: part of the adventure of live training is not knowing the outcome. Using an approach like Zúme always gives you the very same outcome. It's predictable — with 100% certainty.

If you'd like to imagine what a week-long live training schedule would be like, you could check out an example of a training manual like Curtis Sergeant's MetaCamp guidebook. Find a copy online at https://www.dropbox.com/s/w86ri997qsgs529/MetaCamp%20three%20thirds%20version.pdf?oref=e&n=25482097. Read more about his training at https://metacamp.org/.

Eric D (name withheld for security's sake) provided a sample schedule for a week-long training.

Table 4: Sample Schedule for a Week-Long Training

Day	Time	Type	Session
Mon	8:00		Arrival/Registration
Mon	8:30	Teaching	Overview
Mon	9:15	Teaching	Be a disciple worth reproducing
Mon	10:00		Break
Mon	10:15	Application	Introductions & Response
Mon	11:50	Demo	C2J
Mon	12:00		Lunch
Mon	1:00	Teaching	Intro to 3/3rds
Mon	1:20	Application	3/3rds Groups
Mon	3:00		Break
Mon	3:15	Application	Demonstration of movement
Mon	4:30	Teaching	People Profiles
Mon	5:00	Application	CPM Principles & Group Response
Mon	5:30		Dismiss
Mon		Application	Journaling

Day	Time	Type	Session
Tue	8:00		Arrive/Quiet Time
Tue	8:30	Teaching	CPM Principles
Tue	9:00	Application	SOAPS
Tue	10:00		Break
Tue	10:15	Application	3/3rds Groups
Tue	11:50	Demo	C2J
Tue	12:00		Lunch
Tue	1:00	Application	Prayer Wheel
Tue	2:00	Teaching	Writing & Polishing Your Story
Tue	2:20	Application	Practice Your Story
Tue	3:00		Break
Tue	3:15	Teaching	Prayer Walking
Tue	4:00		Travel to PW sites
Tue	4:30	Application	Prayer Walking in Pairs
Tue	5:45		Travel back to Emerald Hills
Tue	6:15	Application	Dinner: Debrief Prayer Walking
Tue	7:00	Teaching	CPM Principles
Tue	7:30	Application	Name List
Tue	8:00		Dismiss
Wed	8:00		Arrival/Quiet Time
Wed	8:30	Teaching	CPM Principles
Wed	9:00	Application	CHAT
Wed	10:00		Break
Wed	10:15	Application	3/3rds Groups
Wed	11:50	Demo	C2J
Wed	12:00		Lunch
Wed	1:00	Teaching	Gospel Tool
Wed	1:20	Application	Practice Gospel Tool
Wed	2:00	Teaching	People of Peace
Wed	3:00		Break
Wed	3:15	Teaching	Shema Lifestyle
Wed	3:45	Application	Practice Shema Statements
Wed	4:30	Teaching	Persecution

Day	Time	Type	Session
Wed	5:30		Dismiss
Wed			Journaling
Thur	8:00		Arrive/Quiet Time
Thur	8:30	Teaching	CPM Principles
Thur	9:15	Application	Group Response
Thur	10:00		Break
Thur	10:15	Application	3/3rds Groups
Thur	11:50	Demo	C2J
Thur	12:00		Lunch
Thur	1:00	Teaching	CPM Principles
Thur	1:30	Application	Group Response
Thur	2:00	Teaching	Master Planning
Thur	2:30	Application	Master Planning (Next 90 days)
Thur	3:00		Break
Thur	3:15	Application	Master Planning (Next 90 days)
Thur	3:45	Application	Prayer (plans & pw)
Thur	4:15		Travel to PW sites
Thur	4:30	Application	Prayer Walking in Pairs
Thur	6:00		Travel back to Emerald Hills
Thur	6:15		Dinner
Thur	7:00		Debrief Prayer Walking
Thur	8:00		Dismiss
Fri	8:00		Arrive/Quiet Time
Fri	8:30		Praise
Fri	9:00		Next 90 Days/Plans
Fri	9:30		Synthesize
Fri	11:30		Commissioning
Fri	12:00		Lunch
Fri	1:00		Depart

Some trainers have begun offering two-day workshops to whet the appetites of would-be disciple-multipliers. Although it's impossible to cover everything adequately in two days, the thinking is that two days is better than none, especially when many interested individuals will likely never be able to arrange for an entire week off of work to attend a full week of CPM/DMM training.

Questions for Discussion:

1. This chapter provides several formats for introducing CPM/ DMM strategies in your church or in the place where you hope to make disciples. Imagine for a moment... why would you think the author would offer these formats? What were his intentions? In your opinion, are those intentions valid? Most importantly, how effective would you say his proposed formats might be in your church or in the place where you hope to make disciples?

2. Evaluate the question: "Is it sneaky to start the organic way?" (In other words, must we gain the approval of our church or organization's leaders in order to experiment/experience CPM/ DMM approaches?)

3. In your opinion, does the multiplicative approach remind you of network marketing? How is it similar? How is it different? Does it bother you to think of Jesus as asking us to "market" (i.e., persuade people to follow) the Good News? Why or why not?

4. In your experience, where do these ever-expanding chains break down? In other words, offer some guesses as to what might sabotage a movement.

5. Based on your learning style, would you rather be involved in a "live training" with an "expert" (an experienced disciple-maker) or would you be comfortable using a web-driven tool like Zúme as your learning approach? Explain.

CHAPTER 12

TOOLS AND TIPS FOR IMPLEMENTERS

There are really no shortcuts with CPM/DMM. For effective multiplication, we have to become real disciples worth multiplying. However, that's not to say we can't list here some patterns we see recurring in the lives of those who have been fruitful in previous case studies. Here are some of those patterns listed as ideas for all of us to consider when hoping to launch a new CPM/DMM. (Most of these tools are from the Zúme course and are highlighted in Zúme videos or audios. To learn more, browse to www.ZúmeProject.com.)

List of 100

In Matthew 28, Jesus said to go and make disciples. His followers did just that. They went to their families. They went to their friends. They went to people they knew in town. They went to people they worked with. They went. Jesus said "Go." They obeyed. Furthermore, God's family grew. God has already given us the relationships we need to "go and make disciples." These are our families, friends, neighbors, co-workers, and classmates - people we've known all our lives, people we've just met. Being faithful

Photo 30: God has already given us a circle of relationships.

with the people God has already put in our lives is a great first step in multiplying disciples. It can start with the simple step of making a list. A list of 100 is a simple tool in the Zúme Toolkit that multiplies disciples. So, specifically, what do we do? We make a list of 100 people in our lives — then we pray for them. Out to the right of each name, place a mark to designate whether the friend/associate is a follower of Jesus or not. You can also specify if you just don't know. Either way, lift up each person on your list. If the friend is not yet a follower, ask God to open his/her heart. Pray that the person will have a dream that will make him/her curious about Christ. Pray specifically for ideas and opportunities to share God's story or your story with each of the people on your list. Pick out the first 5 people and focus on them in particular. Look with full interest in discovering some way of sharing with them during the next 72 hours. When God opens a door, be ready to respond with one of the other tools below.

Creation to Judgment

One of the most significant ways you can help launch a CPM/DMM is to get many people telling the Good News (the gospel) to everyone in their lives and everyone they meet – at least as much as possible. Obviously, this is easier for some people than it is for others. But at least, make sure everyone is prepared to give an answer about the hope that is within him or her (1 Peter 3:15). There are many ways to share God's story. The best way will depend on the person with whom you are sharing and his/her life experiences and view of the world. God uses hearts willing to share to work on hearts willing to hear. It's His work. He just invites us to join in.

One way to share God's Story is by explaining what's happened from God's Creation to His Judgment at the end of this age. When we tell God's story in this way, we can make it long, short, detailed, or just broad strokes, but always connected to the culture of the one who hears. To help tell His Story across different cultures and world views, you can also use hand motions that make it easier to learn and teach. Here is one version of God's Story of Good News (sometimes referred to as Creation to Judgment or C2J). You can also see a version of this story on YouTube, being delivered by "JED" from Team Expansion, at the following website: https://www.youtube.com/watch?v=RetBxWLbDNs.)

Creation to Judgment: In the beginning, God made the whole world and everything in it. He created the first man and the first woman. He placed them in a beautiful garden. He made them part of His family and had a close relationship with them. He created them to live forever. There was no such thing as death. Even in this perfect place, man rebelled against God and brought sin and suffering into the world. God banished man from the garden. The relationship between man and God was broken. Now man would have to face death. Over many hundreds of years, God kept sending messengers into the world. They reminded man of his sin but also told him of God's faithfulness and promise to send a Savior into the world. The Savior would restore the close relationship between God and Man. The Savior would rescue man from death. The Savior would give eternal life and be with man forever. God loves us so much that when the time was right, He sent His Son into the world to be that Savior. Jesus was God's Son. He was born into the world through a virgin. He lived a perfect life. He never sinned. Jesus taught people about God. He performed many miracles showing His great power. He cast out many demons. He healed many people. He made the blind see. He made the deaf hear. He made the lame walk. Jesus even raised the dead. Many religious leaders were threatened and jealous of Jesus. They wanted Him killed. Since He never sinned, Jesus did not have to die. However, He chose to die as a sacrifice for all of us. His painful death covered up the sins of mankind. After this, Jesus was buried in a tomb. God saw the sacrifice Jesus made and accepted it. God showed His acceptance by raising Jesus from the dead on the third day. God said that if we believe and receive Jesus's sacrifice for our sins – if we turn away from our sins and follow Jesus, God cleans us from all sin and welcomes us back into His family. God sends the Holy Spirit to live inside us and make us able to follow Jesus. We are baptized in water to show and seal this restored relationship. As a symbol of death we are buried beneath the water. As a symbol of new life we are raised out of the water to follow Jesus. When Jesus rose from the dead, He spent 40 days on earth. Jesus taught His followers to go everywhere and tell the good news of His salvation to everyone around the world. Jesus said - Go and make disciples of all nations, baptizing them in the name of the Father, Son and Holy Spirit; and teaching them to obey all I have commanded. I will be with you always - even to the end of this age. Jesus was then taken up before their eyes into heaven. One day, Jesus will come again in the same way He left. He will punish forever those who did not love and obey Him. He will receive and reward forever those who did love and obey Him. We will live forever with Him in a new heaven and on a new earth. I believed and received the sacrifice Jesus made for my sins. He has made me clean and restored me as part of God's family. He loves me, and I love Him and will live with Him forever in His kingdom. God loves you and wants you to receive this gift, as well. Would you like to do that right now?"

3 Circles: An Alternate Version of the Good News

Because the Creation to Judgment (C2J) story is rather difficult for some people to learn, some prefer learning a different presentation that has come to be called "3 Circles Life Conversation." It was originally developed by Family Church in West Palm Beach, Florida. They've gone on record saying that it "contributed to tripling their baptisms from 80 in 2013 to 240 in 2014 (Campbell, 2016). The following script is an adaptation of that same story, written in such a way that you can tell the entire 3 Circles Life Conversation story in just 3 minutes (Team Expansion, 2018):

You know, the reality is - **all of us live in this broken world** (*draw a circle on the right side of your paper with lines that show brokenness*). We only have to turn on the news to see suffering, death, war, disease, addictions. It's everywhere, isn't it?	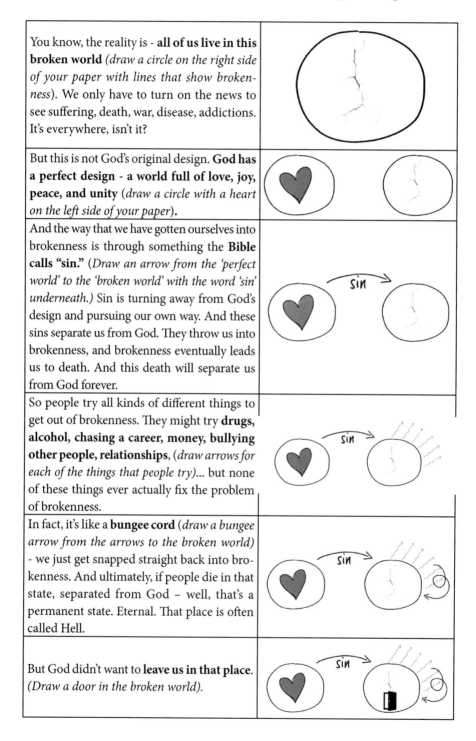
But this is not God's original design. **God has a perfect design - a world full of love, joy, peace, and unity** (*draw a circle with a heart on the left side of your paper*).	
And the way that we have gotten ourselves into brokenness is through something the **Bible calls "sin."** (*Draw an arrow from the 'perfect world' to the 'broken world' with the word 'sin' underneath.*) Sin is turning away from God's design and pursuing our own way. And these sins separate us from God. They throw us into brokenness, and brokenness eventually leads us to death. And this death will separate us from God forever.	
So people try all kinds of different things to get out of brokenness. They might try **drugs, alcohol, chasing a career, money, bullying other people, relationships,** (*draw arrows for each of the things that people try*)... but none of these things ever actually fix the problem of brokenness.	
In fact, it's like a **bungee cord** (*draw a bungee arrow from the arrows to the broken world*) - we just get snapped straight back into brokenness. And ultimately, if people die in that state, separated from God – well, that's a permanent state. Eternal. That place is often called Hell.	
But God didn't want to **leave us in that place.** (*Draw a door in the broken world*).	

125

God loved us so much that He sent Jesus to make a way out for us. **Jesus came down to earth to put an end to our brokenness.** *(Draw another circle at the bottom of your paper and print Jesus at the top of the circle).* In fact, He willingly entered our brokenness to restore God's perfect design.	
How did He do this? By living a perfect life, Jesus took our place in death and **died on a cross** *(draw a cross in the Jesus circle)* as our sacrifice. And God saw this as acceptable, allowing Jesus's sacrifice to account for our brokenness.	
So, it **cancelled out our sin** *(cross out the word sin)!* Jesus CRUSHED IT!	
But three days after **He died** *(draw an arrow pointing down on the left side of the cross)*, **He rose from the dead** *(draw an arrow pointing up on the right side of the cross)*. By **doing so** *(draw a crown on top of the Jesus circle)*,	

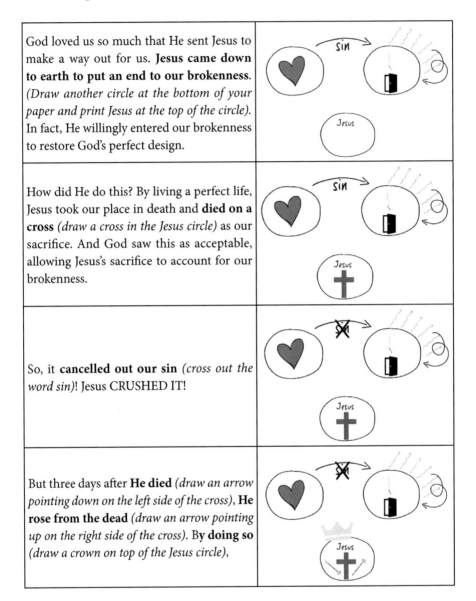

...He made a way out of brokenness for us (*draw an arrow from the broken world pointing to the Jesus circle*). God said that if we **turn** (*write the word 'turn'*) from our sin and **believe** (*write the word 'believe'*) that Jesus died for us, we can leave brokenness, be buried with him through **baptism** (*write the words 'be baptized'*) into his death, in order that, just as Christ was raised, we, too, may live a new life	
so that we can **grow** (*draw an arrow from the Jesus circle to the 'heart' circle and write the word 'grow'*) in a relationship with God and be restored back into His original design along with a community of friends following Christ, and because of Christ, we'll never be alone again.	
Christ has called us to **go** (*draw an arrow pointing from the 'heart' circle to the 'broken-ness' circle and write the word 'go'*) as a community of friends - to be sent, just like Jesus was sent, back into brokenness to help still others come through Him to pursue God's design. We can become like a brand new creation. A new person in Christ.	
So there are really only two kinds of people in the world - there are people who are pursuing God's design (*draw a happy face in the 'heart' circle*)...	
and people who are still in brokenness (*draw a sad face in the 'broken' world*). So we have to ask ourselves, "Where are we?" I'm wondering, "Where do you think you are? Where would you like to be?"	

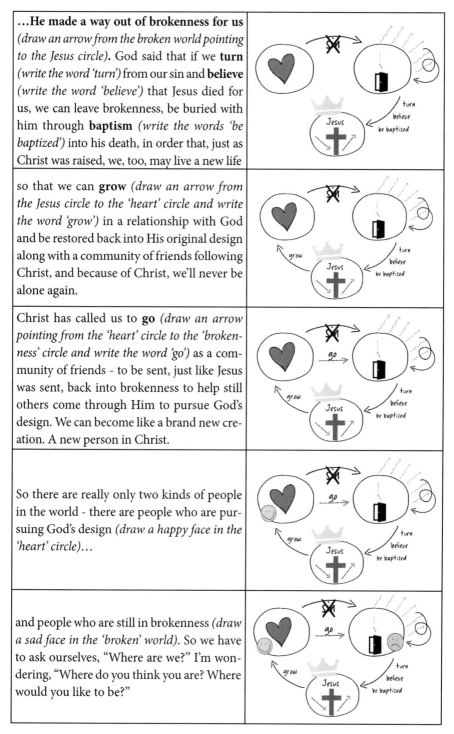

Baptism

Jesus said to go and make disciples of all nations, **baptizing** them in the name of the Father and of the Son and of the Holy Spirit… Baptism - or "Baptizo" in the original language - means a drenching or submerging - like when you dye a cloth and it soaks in the color and comes out transformed. Baptism is a picture of new life, soaked in the image of Jesus, transformed in obedience to God. It is a picture of death to sin, just as Jesus died for our sins; a burial of our old way of life, just as Jesus was buried; a rebirth to a new life in Christ, just as Jesus was resurrected and lives today.

If you have never baptized someone, it might seem intimidating, but it shouldn't be. Here are some simple steps.

Find some standing water, deep enough to allow the new disciple to be submerged. This could be a pond, river, lake or ocean. It could be a bathtub or another way to gather water.

Let the disciple hold one of your hands with theirs and you support their back with the other. Ask two questions like these to make sure the believer understands the decision: "Have you received Jesus Christ as your Lord and Savior?" Will you obey and serve Him as your King for the rest of your life?"

If the believer answers "Yes," to both, then say something like this: "Because you've professed your faith in the Lord Jesus, you are now being baptized in the name of the Father, Son, and Holy Spirit." Help him or her lower into the water, submerge completely, and raise him or her back up. You've baptized a new follower of Jesus, a new citizen of heaven, a new child of the Living God. It's time to celebrate!

One of the great things about Zúme is its ability to bring up baptism as a natural part of becoming a disciple worth multiplying. We believe there is strong evidence in the New Testament for baptizing someone early in his or her life as a disciple. Somewhere along the line, some-one began holding back on baptism as if it's some kind of prize to be reserved only for those who have proven their faithfulness. We can't see one example of this behavior in the New Testament. What's more, when explained as a natural part of the belief cycle, baptism can truly increase the believer's commitment and testimony, in addition to completing biblical obedience, as noted above.

Fortunately, we see great examples of this in multiple fields. For example, Mike (pseudonym, because of political sensitivities and the security issues) is a new Team Expansion worker with refugees overseas. He wrote:

Photo 31: Jesus told his followers, "Make disciples, baptizing them."

When we arrived here just a few months ago, I began going to the refugee camp each week, helping with a Zúme course that another worker had started. Even though I was brand new, many of the refugees spoke English because they came from African lands where English is a national language. What's more, Zúme makes it easy to facilitate discussions about a number of important topics that would be difficult to bring up in most any other context. When the group watched the Zúme video about baptism, it prompted an easy discussion on the matter and several in the group admitted they just hadn't thought about baptism before. Because Zúme makes it so natural and easy, they were extremely open to consider it. We made sure they had understood the biblical background for baptism and, last Saturday, five people stood by the sea, shared their testimonies with their friends (another Zúme teaching), then gave their lives to Christ in baptism. One of the testimonies was from a woman who was raised as a Muslim but saw her Christian friends go to church every week. Because her family was Muslim, she was strictly forbidden to go with them. She always wanted to

129

go to church with her childhood friends. As a refugee, she had even been sent to a prison in a nearby country. While in prison, she remembered the way her childhood friends would always tell her that Jesus would help her in hard times. So there, in the darkness of her cell, she cried out to Jesus! Even though she was in prison for several months, she had joy in her heart because she could pray to Jesus! She is now exceedingly grateful for her freedom to worship Him. It was an exciting day!

Spiritual Economy

This is more of a concept than it is a tool. Thus, once we understand the concept, it prompts us to "think differently" about how we implement CPM/DMM principles. You see, in this broken world, people feel rewarded when they take, when they receive, and when they gain more than those around them. In His Scriptures, God tells His people, "For my thoughts are not your thoughts, neither are your ways my ways" (Isaiah 55:8). God shows us in His Kingdom economy we're rewarded not by what we get but by what we give away. God says, "I will save you, and you will be a blessing" (Zechariah 8:13). Jesus said, "It is more blessed to give than to receive" (Acts 20:35). Giving away what God gives us and blessing others when God blesses us is the foundation for the spiritual breathing we learned about before. We breathe in and hear from God. We breathe out and obey what we hear and share with others. When we are faithful to obey and share what the Lord has shared with us, then He promises to share even more. Jesus said, "Whoever can be trusted with very little can also be trusted with much" (Luke 16:10). This is the path to deeper insights, greater intimacy, and living the abundant life God created us to live. This is the way we can walk in the good works God has already planned for us to do. If we want to be rewarded with God's greatest reward, then we have to practice the things that He promises to bless.

We must...

- Obey and share
- Do and teach
- Practice and pass on

...everything that God tells us to do. If we want others to receive God's greatest reward, then we have to show them how to do the same thing, too. This is a major part of being a disciple and a major part of making disciples.

- We are followers and leaders
- We are learners and teachers
- We are blessed and we are a blessing

God doesn't want us to wait until we know everything before we start obeying and sharing. That day will never come. God doesn't expect us to be fully mature before we start multiplying. He wants us to multiply right away. God wants us to obey what we already know and to share what we've already heard. Then He wants us to teach others to do the same. After all, that's obeying and sharing what He's already told us to do. This is the path to maturity and growth.

Photo 32: God wants us to multiply right away.

Three-Minute Testimony ("My Story")

Jesus told His followers, "You are witnesses of these things" (Luke 24:48). As followers of Jesus, we are "witnesses," too, "testifying" about the impact Jesus has had on our lives. Your story of your relationship with God is called your testimony. Everybody has a story. This is a chance to practice yours. Choose one or two followers with whom to practice. Then pick five names from your list of 100. Make sure you choose people in the category "non-Christian" or "unknown spiritual status." Practice your testimony, your story of Jesus, by having your practice partners pretend to be one of the five people you chose from your list. Practice shaping your story to make it specific for each of the five. You should be able to share a short version of your story in about three minutes. There are endless ways to shape your story, but here are some ways that we've seen work well with others:

- You can share a simple statement about why you chose to follow Jesus. This works well for a brand new believer.
- You can share your "before" and "after" story - what your life was like before you knew Jesus and what your life is like now.
- You can share your "with" and "without" story of what your life is like "with Jesus" and what it would be like "without Him." This version of your story works well if you came to faith at a young age.

When you finish sharing, let your practice partner take his/her turn. Keep going back and forth until you've both finished your five. Want to make an even greater impact? When sharing your story, it's helpful to think of it as part of a three-part process:

- Their story: Ask the person with whom you are talking to share about his/her spiritual journey.
- Your story: Then share your testimony shaped around their experience.
- God's story: Finally share God's story in a way that connects with their worldview, values, and priorities. If you're worried about how to get started, keep it simple. Just share a statement of why you decided to follow Jesus.

God can use your story to change lives; but remember, you're the one who gets to tell it.

It's impossible to overstate how important this tool is for establishing a CPM/DMM. In fact, one well-known missionary/evangelist put it this way, in what came to be known as the Strachan Theorem: "The growth of any movement is in direct proportion to its success in mobilizing its total membership in the constant propagation of its beliefs" (International Bulletin of Missionary Research, 1979).

Greatest Blessing

When someone chooses to follow Jesus, how do you help them move down the right path? How do you help them become a producer in God's Kingdom and not just another consumer? How do you help them receive all the blessings that God is willing to give?

Try starting by telling them this:

- It is a blessing to follow Jesus.
- It is a great blessing to lead others to follow Jesus.
- It is a greater blessing to start a new spiritual family.
- It is the greatest blessing to equip others to start new spiritual families.

Then proceed to tell them, "You have chosen to follow Jesus, and so God has blessed you. I want you to have God's great blessing, greater blessing, and greatest blessing, too. Can I show you how?"

If the new follower wants to know more, ask him or her to make a list of 100 people he/she already knows. Then ask him/her to choose five people from that list - five people who do not know Jesus - five people to share with right away. Explain, "It is a blessing to follow Jesus. Are there others with whom you want to share this blessing?" Teach him/her to share his/her testimony - the story of what God is doing in his or her life. Then be sure also to teach the new follower to share the gospel - the story of what God is doing in the world. Teach him or her how to share about God's great, greater, and greatest blessings. Have him or her practice these things one time for each of the five people with whom the follower has chosen to share. "First, share 'your story.' Then God's story. Then God's blessings."

Each time, role play as one of the five people from the follower's list of 100. Each time, the follower shares his or her story. Then he or she shares God's story. Remind the follower to invite each of the five to become a follower of Jesus, too. In this way, teach each new follower about God's great, greater, and greatest blessing. Each time, ask the new follower questions or make comments that you think each of the five might make. After you practice, ask to meet again in about a week to see how things went when the new follower tried to share with the five. Be sure to follow up. You want to give the new follower enough time to meet with the five, but you don't want to give so much time that he or she puts it off or forgets. Always ask for a phone number or email address or another way to keep in touch. Pray with the new follower that God will give the right words just as he or she has practiced. When you meet a week later, if the new follower hasn't shared, offer to practice with him or her again. You can even offer to go with him or her right then to any of the five who might be available. Do everything you can to help him or her begin sharing. Don't talk about new things. You want to give the new follower the best opportunity to be faithful with what he or she has already learned.

If the new follower refuses or makes excuses, ask God if he or she is really "good soil" that will be fruitful for His kingdom or if there is somewhere else you should be investing. If the new follower shares, then you can celebrate! Even if no one on the list believed, make sure the new follower understands how great it is that he or she heard, obeyed, and shared. That's being faithful. Since the new follower has been faithful with a little, offer to share more. Share about baptism and other tools he or she can use immediately **or** ask the follower to choose some other people from his or her list of 100 - people who don't know or don't follow Jesus. And then start the cycle all over again with more practice. Practice his or her personal story, God's story, and God's blessings. Then pray.

Now if the follower shared **and** someone on his or her list believed, we **really** celebrate! God's family is getting bigger! Make sure the new follower is sharing about the great, greater, and greatest blessing because this is what keeps God's family growing. If he or she didn't share about God's blessings, go over it again — the blessings, how a new follower of Jesus can make a list, how the new follower can share his or her story, share God's story, and share the blessings — all so that the new follower of Jesus can learn and share, too. After you've practiced, send the new follower back to any new believers so he or she can continue sharing with them, too.

Duckling Discipleship

Have you ever seen a group of ducklings out for a walk? No matter where you are in the world, it always looks the same.

Photo 33: Disciples follow like ducklings or, in this case, goslings.

A mother duck leads, and her ducklings follow, one by one, all in a row. The mother duck leads. The little ducks follow. However, if you look more closely, you'll see something else is happening, too. Each little duckling is actually playing two roles - at exactly the same time. Each little duckling is a **follower** because it's following the mother duck or another duckling that's walking right in front of it. And, at exactly the same time, each little duckling is a **leader** because it's leading the duckling (or ducklings) walking right behind it. So is the duckling a follower or a leader? Yes. It's both. That's why ducks "out for a walk" have everything to do with making disciples. God wants His family to grow far, and so He expects every follower to be a leader, every believer to be a sharer, and every disciple to be a disciple-maker - at exactly the same time. One of the traps we fall into, as disciples and disciple-makers, is the false belief that we have to know everything, or even just a lot of things, before we share anything. That's not how discipleship works.

Disciples are like ducklings. To be a leader, they don't have to know everything. They just have to be one step ahead. God wants His family to grow in faithfulness - and so He expects every leader to be a follower, every sharer to be a believer, and every disciple-maker to be a disciple - at exactly the same time, too.

Another trap we fall into, as disciples and disciple-makers, is the false belief that someone, somewhere knows everything, and, if we just find and follow that someone, then we're set. That's not how discipleship works, either. In God's Kingdom, there's only one "mother duck" that all of us follow — and that's Jesus Christ. No missionary. No pastor. No seminary professor. Only Jesus deserves the full measure of our faith. The rest of us are "in process." There will always be someone closer to Jesus that we can follow. There will always be someone farther away that we can lead. Either way, our eyes and our hearts should always be fully fixed on Jesus. In the Bible, Paul, who wrote much of the New Testament and started many of the first churches, didn't just write, "Follow me." He wrote, "Follow my example, as I follow the example of Christ" (1 Corinthians 11:1). Paul knew what ducklings everywhere know and what every disciple should know, too - every leader in God's Kingdom has to be a follower - and all of us follow Jesus. In the Bible, Paul also wrote, "And the things you have heard me say in the presence of many witnesses entrust to reliable people who will also be qualified to teach others" (2 Timothy 2:2). Every follower in God's Kingdom has to be a leader - and all of us should lead like Jesus, laying down our lives for others. If you want to see God's family grow far and grow in faithfulness, then think of disciple-making like ducklings - become a follower and a leader at exactly the same time.

Eyes to See

As humans, we think about, focus on, and work for things that we can see. We call it reality, the way things are. The kingdom grows more quickly when we open our eyes to the places where the kingdom hasn't ventured yet. There are places all around us where God's will is not being done on earth as it is in heaven - giant gaps where brokenness, pain, persecution, suffering, and death are a part of normal, everyday life. Every disciple and every follower of Jesus needs to be able to see not just where God's Kingdom is, but where God's Kingdom isn't. Kingdom work is about entering into those gaps and into those dark places and working to close the chasms and bring light and life during our time here on earth.

We can see where God's Kingdom isn't in two ways: through people we already know and through people we haven't yet met. The first way is through people we already know - our **ongoing relationships** of friends and family, co-workers, classmates, neighbors, and more. This is the way God's Story travels **fastest**. We love and care about these people because we know them already. It's natural. Jesus told a story of a selfish rich man, arrogant in life, and now being punished in hell. The rich man says, "Then I beg you, father, send Lazarus to my family, for I have five brothers. Let him warn them, so that they will not also come to this place of torment" (Luke 16:27-28). Jesus showed us how even the selfish and suffering have some love and concern for those close to them. The people we know are placed in our lives because God loves us and wants us to love them. We need to be good stewards of those relationships with love, patience, and persistence. Disciples multiply when they're concerned for the people God's placed around them and they have a plan to do something about it. You can help increase their care and build a simple plan to multiply in just a few steps.

For the followers, disciples can equip and encourage them to be more fruitful and faithful. For the non-followers, disciples can learn how to share and introduce them to a loving God. For those about whom they're not sure, disciples can learn to invest their time and learn more.

There's also a way we see where God's Kingdom isn't through people we haven't met. These are people **outside our relationships,** people we don't know, neighbors to whom we've never said more than "hello," businessmen and women we pass on the street, strangers in every village, town, or city we've never yet visited. Jesus said to make disciples of all nations. Jesus said, "You will be my witnesses in Jerusalem, and in all Judea and Samaria, and to the ends of the earth" (Acts 1:8).

Sharing with people we know is the way God's Story travels fastest. Sharing with people we don't know yet is the way God's Story travels farthest. If we love and care about these people we don't know, that's not natural. It's supernatural and evidence of the Holy Spirit at work in our lives. God's favorites are the least, the last, and the lost. These are the ones to whom He pours out His heart over and over again. These are the ones in whom we have to invest our lives. God commands us to go. And part of going is to go not just to those who are close by but also to those who live in the spiritually darkest corners of the world, to people who sometimes have never even heard the name of Jesus.

Photo 34: Lord, give us eyes to see into the darkness, where the Kingdom isn't.

God's Word says, "God resists the proud, but gives grace to the humble" (James 4:6). As followers of Jesus we must give grace as He gives it - to the humble, to the desperate, and to the lost. Disciples multiply when they're concerned for the people God's placed in their lives. Disciples multiply even more when they're concerned for the people God's placed nowhere near them. But even then, they still need a plan. You can help increase a disciple's care for others and build a simple plan to multiply by training them to look for the people God's already prepared to hear.

Jesus said, "When you enter a house, first say, 'Peace to this house.' If someone who promotes peace is there, your peace will rest on them; if not, it will return to you" (Luke 10:5-6). We call someone whom God has already prepared to hear a **person of peace** - someone responsive to God's message and faithful in **obeying** and **sharing** with others. In a place where we know very few, instead of sharing with our friends, families, co-workers, classmates, and neighbors, we train a person of peace how to reach his or her relationships. However, the best results always come when we focus on the faithful. Remember, faithfulness is demonstrated by **obeying** what God tells us and **sharing** it with others.

Faithful people who obey and share are like the good soil to whom Jesus referred. Jesus said, "Still other seed fell on good soil, where it produced a crop–a hundred, sixty or thirty times what was sown" (Matthew 13:8).

Faithful people don't have hard hearts that reject God's Word. They don't fall away when they're persecuted or when times get hard. **They aren't distracted by the worries of this world or riches that don't last.** Faithful people are like the demon-possessed man in the Gerasenes who obeyed and shared what Jesus showed him. In his case, one man who obeyed and shared produced many, many people who wanted to know more about Jesus. Opening our eyes to see where the Kingdom isn't and reaching out through people we know and people we don't know yet is how disciples multiply and God's Kingdom grows far and fast.

Lord's Supper

Jesus said, "I am the living bread that came down from heaven. Whoever eats this bread will live forever. This bread is my flesh, which I will give for the life of the world" (John 6:51). Holy Communion or "The Lord's Supper" is a way to celebrate our intimate connection and ongoing relationship with Jesus. Here's a simple way to celebrate:

When you gather as followers of Jesus, spend time in quiet meditation, silently considering and confessing your sins. Have someone read this passage from Scripture: "For I received from the Lord what I also passed on to you: The Lord Jesus, on the night he was betrayed, took bread, and when he had given thanks, he broke it and said, 'This is my body, which is for you; do this in remembrance of me.'" (1 Corinthians 11:23-24). Pass out bread you have set aside for your group and eat.

Continue the reading: "In the same way, after supper he took the cup, saying, 'This cup is the new covenant in my blood; do this, whenever you drink it, in remembrance of me'" (1 Corinthians 11:25). Share the juice or wine you have set aside for your group and drink. Finish the reading: "For whenever you eat this bread and drink this cup, you proclaim the Lord's death until he comes" (1 Corinthians 11:26).

You have shared in the Lord's Supper. Celebrate in prayer or singing - you are His and He is yours!

Training Cycle

The **Training Cycle** helps disciples go from one to many and turns a mission into a movement. Have you ever learned how to ride a bicycle? Have you ever helped someone else learn? If so, chances are you already know the **Training Cycle**. It's as easy as MAWL: **model, assist, watch, and leave**. Think back - before you ever rode a bicycle, you probably saw someone else ride one first. That's **modeling**. Model, assist, watch, and leave.

Modeling is simply showing someone else an example of how it's done. When a child first sees someone else riding a bike, they get the idea right away. Modeling is like that – it doesn't have to be done often, and usually it only needs to be done once. Think back to that first bike ride. Did you want to just watch? Or were you excited to get on and give it a try? What if nobody ever gave you the chance? Too much modeling can actually hurt the training process. **Modeling** is about showing someone just a little - and then giving them a try.

So what happened on that first ride? Did they just give you the bicycle and walk away? Probably not. When most people learn how to ride a bike, someone is right there for the first few pedals. Walking along side and keeping you on track. That's **assisting**. **Model, assist, watch, and leave**. Assisting is allowing a learner to practice a skill but making sure the falls aren't too hard. Assisting takes longer than modeling. But not too long. It requires some hand-holding, some direction, and some coaching, but it's just about passing on the basics. It's not about getting someone to perfect. It's about getting them to pedal. Can you imagine someone running alongside you as you started to pedal fast and gain some speed? They wouldn't last long, and you'd never learn to keep your balance. **Assisting** is about getting someone going and allowing them to steer a little on their own. When they start to move, they're actually modeling for the next learner on the way.

Even when no one else's hands are on the bike, it doesn't mean you're all alone. Usually there's someone keeping an eye out - but from a distance. That's watching. Model, assist, watch, and leave. Watching is influencing a learner until he/she is competent in that skill, all without having to step in and take control. In bike riding, someone can get up and going fairly quickly, but that doesn't mean he/she knows all the rules of the road. Watching is about making sure someone's going to be safe - even when no one's around. Watching is about making sure not just that someone knows what to do, but also that they'll do it - even when no one's looking. In this phase of the Training Cycle, the learner will grow and teach others how to grow... so they teach others how to grow... so they teach others how to grow. Disciples make disciples who make disciples who make disciples. All the way down to the third and fourth generation. Watching is about making sure a learner matures and is not just willing but also able to help others. Watching takes a while. It may take ten times as long as modeling and assisting combined. It may be longer. The wait is always worth it.

Eventually, the rider just rides the bike. That's what **leaving** is all about. **Model, assist, watch, and**

Photo 35: Did you ever watch someone learning to ride a bike?

leave. Leaving is like a graduation. (In fact, instead of saying "leaving," some people like to use the word, "launching.") A student becomes a teacher. A worker becomes a co-worker. A disciple becomes a friend. In bike riding, the one who teaches you to ride doesn't go along for every ride you take. At times they may ride with you. At times you ride separately, or with others, or alone. **Leaving** is about giving one last gift to someone you love - the gift of freedom. Leaving is about equipping someone to go where you've already gone but also encouraging them to go where you haven't gotten to yet.

Model, assist, watch, and leave. From one to many. From a mission to a movement.

Leadership Cells

In a true movement, you need something to prepare followers in a very short time to become leaders for a lifetime. One becomes two. Two become four. Four become eight. Individual multiplication brings on generational increase which, in turn, ushers in exponential growth.

This is the model God built into His creation. This is the way God intends His family to grow. We've already learned the 3/3 pattern that turns consumers into producers, learners into leaders, and disciples into disciple-makers. Look Back - Look Up - Look Forward. Learn - Obey - Share. This way of meeting together produces ongoing spiritual growth in individual believers and ongoing reproductive growth in a group of followers of Jesus. This pattern helps disciples multiply.

But what if a group is together for only a short period of time? Can they still grow and reproduce God's Kingdom? Leadership Cells are a way to put the 3/3 pattern to work when you know there's a limit to how long a group can be together. Leadership Cells equip individual believers in a short time to learn reproductive patterns that last a life-time. Leadership Cells help learners become leaders who will then start new groups, train new churches, and begin more Leadership Cells to grow God's family. Leadership Cells learn well when a group is mobile. Nomads, students, military personnel, and seasonal workers who already follow Jesus work great in a Leadership Cell. Because of their culture, their profession, or their season of life, they may have a hard time establishing an ongoing group, but they can absolutely be trained how to start groups in each place they travel. Leadership Cells also work well when a group of people come to faith at the same time. A family, a network of friends, or even a small village can be trained in a short time to become producers for a lifetime even without individual follow-ups or spiritual coaching.

However, as we've mentioned before, our goal is not merely to conduct training sessions. If all we ever do is conduct Leadership Cells, we'll do lots of training, but we won't have a CPM/DMM. For that to happen, we have to start **churches**, even if they're "**simple churches**." So, bottom line, celebrate the start-up of another Leadership Cell. More than that, **celebrate when leaders start churches, too**.

Non-Sequential

For a CPM or DMM to happen, we need to break the habit of thinking in a linear pattern as a way of accelerating kingdom growth. To make disciples who make disciples more quickly, we have to keep in mind that multiple things can happen at the same time, and there is not a certain order in which they need to happen. We have to learn the power of **non-sequential** growth.

When people think about disciples multiplying, they often think of it as a step-by-step process or sequence like this:

1. Prayer
2. Preparation
3. Sharing God's good news
4. Building disciples
5. Building churches
6. Developing leader
7. Reproduction

When we learn this way, kingdom growth seems to be an easy-to-follow, linear and sequential process. One problem is that's not how it always works. A bigger problem is that's not how it of-

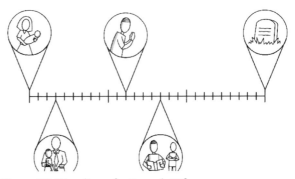

Figure 36. Timeline of a Person's Life

ten works best. Imagine a line that represents a person's life (see Figure 36. Timeline of a Person's Life).

Imagine we plot a person's birth, the point in time when the person first hears God's good news, the point that the person first chooses to follow Jesus, the point that the person first shares his or her story and God's story, the point that the person first begins to multiply, and the point when the person's earthly

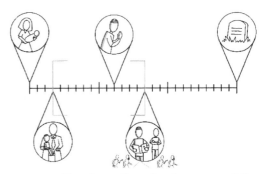

Figure 37. Timeframe from first hearing until first sharing the Good News.

life ends. So from first hearing about Jesus until first sharing about Jesus is what we could consider a spiritual generation (the amount of time before multiplying). This is essentially the amount of time before God's family grows. We could draw it on the graph (see Figure 37. Timeframe from first hearing until first sharing the Good News.).

This is how discipleship is usually taught. When we use a pattern like greatest blessing, note what happens. Now a new disciple starts multiplying immediately. The spiritual generation shortens. Someone hears God's good news sooner. God's family grows more quickly. More people are saved for eternity. All of it - simply by moving when they multiply. What if we keep going? What if someone starts multiplying even earlier? What if they begin to share after they first hear instead of after they first believe? See how the time shortens (see Figure 38. The spiritual generation shortens when we start multiplying immediately.)?

Some are open to gathering a group and sharing what they learn from God's Word with friends and family before they ever say "yes" to Jesus. If we show those people how to gather a group, share what they learn, and show others how to do the same, God's family grows even faster. Now discipleship is a path to Jesus, not just something we share after salvation. We might draw it like this (see Figure 39. Sharing about Jesus before we ever say "yes" to Jesus.). This is a way a family or friends or even a village can come to follow Jesus. What if someone can multiply even sooner?

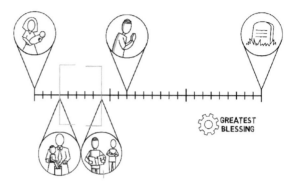

Figure 38. The spiritual generation shortens when we start multiplying immediately.

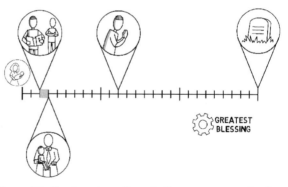

Figure 39. Sharing about Jesus before we ever say "yes" to Jesus.

even sooner? What if someone could share God's ways before he or she even meets God's Son? Sometimes a group may be unable or not ready to hear God's good news immediately. However, this group can still learn God's patterns through efforts like community development or leadership training. This group can begin multiplying God's patterns:

learning, obeying, sharing, and teaching others to do the same even before they first hear about Jesus. When this happens, God's ways are imprinted into willing hearts. His patterns are woven into a community and individual lives. Then when God has prepared His way - God's good news can reveal the truth they've been receiving all along. This is the way an institution, a community, or even a country can come to follow Jesus.

Non-sequential growth still requires that we ask what's essential. No matter what process, the biggest question is always the same - Who is the good soil that will be faithful? Who will learn and practice and share God's ways? Uncovering this good soil, discovering these good hearts, is worth all of our time and energy and effort. These are the ones to whom we pour out our hearts. These are the ones for whom we pour out our lives. These are the ones who grow God's Kingdom best.

Pace

Multiplying matters. Multiplying quickly matters even more. We've already mentioned the pace of multiplication. We presented the topic as a reason why we might want to consider CPM/DMM strategies and life practices in the first place. We are discussing the pace of growth again because this time we're considering rapid multiplication as a characteristic of a healthy church and of healthy disciples. Why?

Pace is about time, how quickly or slowly things happen. Pace matters because where we all spend our eternity, an existence that outlasts time, is determined in the short time we call "life." God's Word tells us, "Instead he is patient with you, not wanting anyone to perish, but everyone to come to repentance" (2 Peter 3:9). God gives us more time because He knows we only have a short time to do all He's called us to do and to reach all He's called us to reach. To follow Jesus more closely, we have to pursue His people more quickly. We can't just take our time. We have to increase our **pace**. The global church, all followers of Jesus together, is larger than it's ever been. The global church, all followers of Jesus, together, is a larger portion of the world's population than ever before. However, even with those large numbers, the global church is not growing faster than the global population. That means that while there are more of us who follow Jesus than ever before, there are even more who are not following Jesus and will spend their eternity separated from Him.

Making disciples who multiply matters. Start with just one disciple. If that one disciple multiplies and makes a new disciple once every 18 months, an entire year and a half, and then those disciples do the same, in 10 years there will be 64 new followers of Jesus. Sixty-four people will spend their forever with a loving God. That represents a 6300% increase in the number of disciples!

But what if they moved a little faster? What if they increased their **pace**? If they multiply now in four months, one-third of a year instead of 18 months, and those disciple do the same, in 10 years there will now be a billion new followers of Jesus. Instead of less than 100, there will be more than 1,000,000,000. All by increasing PACE. Going from 18 months to four months means we're moving four-and-a-half times faster. When that acceleration is applied to every disciple over the course of 10 years, it would result in a 99,999,993,600% increase for God's family! Less than a hundred. More than a billion. Pace matters!

Pace matters. Sharing our story and God's story and leading someone to follow Jesus grows God's family. Sharing with a new follower how to do exactly the same grows God's family like a wildfire - like yeast through a loaf. All because of **pace**.

Leadership in Networks

In a CPM/DMM, once we are able to start a growing group of small churches, we need to help them work together. They need to learn to grow new leaders and accomplish even more of the good things God has planned for His people. So, thinking long-term, what happens to churches as they grow and start new churches that start new churches that start new churches? How do they stay connected? How do they live life together as an extended spiritual family? The answer is that all of these simple churches are just like the cells in a growing body, and they connect and network into a city or regional church. The churches are related. They share the same spiritual DNA. They are all connected out of the same first multiplying family. Now, with some guidance, they come together as a larger body to do even more.

At the city and regional level, God's Word shows that the growing body of believers is served by a new group of leaders. In the New Testament, the church calls these servants elders and deacons, shepherds and overseers of the flock. We learn in God's Word that the multitude of small home churches in the city of Jerusalem was served by a group of seven servants or deacons. We learn in God's Word that the multitude of home churches in the city of Ephesus were served by a small group of elders, shepherds, who were to follow the model of the Good Shepherd Jesus and lay down their lives for their flocks. In the city or region, we also see a group of five leadership gifts given. God's Word says, "So Christ himself gave the apostles, the prophets, the evangelists, the pastors and teachers, to equip his people for works of service, so that the body of Christ may be built up" (Ephesians 4:11-12). These spiritual gifts were given not so a small group could do all the work of the church but so they could serve and prepare the followers of Jesus to do the work so the whole body of believers could work together to accomplish all God has in His heart to do. In addition to, or in place of, meeting with their own spiritual families, these leaders met, prayed, fellowshipped, and encouraged one another in much the same way that any simple church in a home would.

The 3/3 pattern is used in leadership training meetings and peer mentoring. Another tool or pattern, Four Fields, is used for planning, evaluation, and coaching at higher levels just as it is at the local level. (We mentioned this valuable tool in Chapter 11.)

When the leaders meet, they share what is happening not only as individuals but also across their networks. They represent the families and share about the well-being of the ones they serve. A good place for a network of spiritual families to center is the place where that network starts. A church network that launches from Tampa will start as a city church in Tampa. As they grow and serve throughout the state, they will act on behalf of the network in Florida. As they send and serve around the country and around the world, they begin to function at a national or even international level. Jesus said, "Whoever can be trusted

Photo 40: Leaders of spiritual families can form networks to make a "city church."

with very little can also be trusted with much" (Luke 16:10). These networks of churches remain connected because of their common spiritual DNA and shared beginnings. Sometimes the networks split off into multiple networks based on language, opportunities to meet, or for other reasons. This is a part of growth and not a problem. The willingness of simple churches and individual followers to learn, obey, and share God's Word is the spiritual DNA of a movement. If it is passed on successfully from generation to generation, from church to church, and from believer to believer, then everything needed to begin a new movement of multiplying disciples is already present in every spiritual family and in every follower of Jesus. When movements launch movements, that's when we start to see the "leaven" working through the dough of a city or a state or even a nation. That is how the Kingdom of God comes in such a way that God's will is being done on earth as it is in heaven. That is how we can finish the Great Commission by making disciples of all nations.

Peer Mentoring Groups

Jesus said, "A new command I give you: Love one another. As I have loved you, so you must love one another. By this everyone will know that you are my disciples, if you love one another" (John 13:34-35). A peer mentoring group is a group that consists of people who are leading and starting 3/3 groups. It also follows a 3/3 format and is a powerful way to assess the spiritual health of God's work in your area. Peer mentoring groups use leader-to-leader mentoring with individual followers of Jesus, with simple churches, with ministry organizations, or even with a global simple church network that reaches around the world. Peer mentoring groups follow Jesus's example of ministry from Scripture, ask questions of one another, and give feedback — all using the same basic time structure as a 3/3 group. The purpose of these groups is not to judge nor to lift one member up and tear another down. Jesus said, "Do not judge, or you too will be judged. For in the same way you judge others, you will be judged, and with the measure you use, it will be measured to you" (Matthew 7:1-2). Instead, the purpose of a peer mentoring group is to provide a simple format for helping followers of Jesus grow through prayer, obedience, application, and accountability. In other words — "to love one another."

Here's how it works:

Look Back: During the first third, spend time in prayer and care just like you would in a basic 3/3 group. Then spend time looking at the group's vision. How well are we individually abiding in Jesus as we read Scripture, pray, trust and obey God, and live out key relationships? Finally, during this first third, have the group review and respond to each individual's action plans and commitments made in the last session.

Look Up: The middle third of the group's time is spent looking up for God's wisdom and direction through Scripture, discussion, and prayer. Offer a brief and simple prayer, asking God to teach you His will and His ways through His Word. Ask the Holy Spirit to lead your time. Group members should share what they have learned from the Lord about their area of leadership, either through God's Word, prayer, or from other followers. Have the group discuss the following simple questions:

- How are you doing in each major component of your ministry?
- What is working well? What are your biggest challenges?

- Review your current generational map.
- What challenged you or what did you find hard to understand?
- What is God showing you recently?
- Are there any questions and feedback from seasoned leaders or other participants?

Look Forward: The final third of the group's time is spent looking forward to how we can each apply and obey what we've learned. Spend time in silent prayer with everyone in the group, asking the Holy Spirit to show them how to answer these questions:

- What action plans or goals would God have me put into practice before our next time together?
- How can my mentor or other group members help me in this work?
- Finally, spend time as a group talking to God in prayer. Have the group pray so that each member is prayed for. Ask God to prepare the hearts of all those whom the group will reach out during their time apart. Pray for God to give each member of the group the courage and strength to apply and obey what God has taught him/her in this session. If a seasoned leader needs to pray specifically for a younger leader, this is the perfect time for that prayer. Since these groups often meet at a distance, you are unlikely to be able to celebrate the Lord's Supper or share a meal, but be sure to make time to check in about health, family, and friends. Jesus showed us again and again that, even though He accomplished the most important works, He balanced it, always, with time for the ones He loved.

A peer mentoring group is a simple but strategic tool to develop stronger leaders.

The Need for Resilience and Determination

Like most valuable outcomes, there is a cost to launching Kingdom Movements. Sometimes, the cost is personal. Always, the price includes a large measure of resilience and determination. Sometimes, you will feel as if you are right in the middle of a spiritual battle. We've already pointed to the passage in Ephesians 6, but it deserves to be highlighted again because of the gravity and significance of the battle in which we are engaged. Paul wrote:

Finally, be strong in the Lord and in his mighty power. Put on the full armor of God, so that you can take your stand against the devil's schemes. For our struggle is not against flesh and blood, but against the rulers, against the authorities, against the powers of this dark world and against the spiritual forces of evil in the heavenly realms. Therefore put on the full armor of God, so that when the day of evil comes, you may be able to stand your ground, and after you have done everything, to stand. Stand firm then, with the belt of truth buckled around your waist, with the breastplate of righteousness in place, and with your feet fitted with the readiness that comes from the gospel of peace. In addition to all this, take up the shield of faith, with which you can extinguish all the flaming arrows of the evil one. Take

Photo 41: Launching a movement will require all the determination you can muster.

the helmet of salvation and the sword of the Spirit, which is the word of God. And pray in the Spirit on all occasions with all kinds of prayers and requests. With this in mind, be alert and always keep on praying for all the Lord's people. Pray also for me, that whenever I speak, words may be given me so that I will fearlessly make known the mystery of the gospel, for which I am an ambassador in chains. Pray that I may declare it fearlessly, as I should (Ephesians 6:10-20).

To help us understand the need for determination and resilience, we end with this personal and true testimony from Ryan F. (last name withheld for security's sake).

I can remember the weeks all so clearly. The weather was hot, spiritual conversations were a dead end road, and discouragement was a cloud that continued to thicken around us. Getting a group started was only a dream at that point— I would've been content with just getting the name of Jesus out in a conversation before getting shut down.

My team and I had been walking the streets of a large city in Southern Italy, attempting to live out the disciple-making principles we had so diligently learned. We were experiencing no fruit and felt as if we were moving backwards. I thought for sure I would see the Holy Spirit move more fluidly than what I was seeing. In fact, to me, it seemed the Holy Spirit wasn't moving at all.

A few weeks in, my teammates and I were certain we had found a person of peace; an influential member among young adults, receptive, and curious of the additional stories we had to share. Once we found our man, whom we'll call Russell, we insisted on meeting again the following week and instructed Russell to bring friends. Finally, we were catching traction! Or so we thought.

We had somehow managed to form a 3/3 group with a few guys from West Africa, yet that, too, proved to be a source of discouragement as we could never manage to get through a full study without the dialogue turning into debate. In the subsequent weeks, the same took place. It was at this point that I began to doubt the process and even began to doubt if I was up for the task. Additionally, I questioned, "Does this method really work?" "Had we really found a person of peace?" "Should we just move on?" "If so, how could we move and leave these men's eternities in the lurch?"

Our team met, and we came to the conclusion we would meet one more week to gauge whether or not to continue. However, little did we know, a few members in this group decided to recruit another member who had grown up in an intensely rigorous Islamic household in which his father was a professor of the Quran. For the sake of protecting identity, this man will be referred to as Silas. In essence, Silas did not necessarily know the Quran as absolute truth but rather as a legalistic code for life.

With that, he was exceptionally skilled at trapping Christians. And that is what he did.

At this particular study, the conversation was heightened, and my friend, Silas, was right in the middle of it. We finally had to end the meeting, having agreed to disagree. We stated, "Silas, this is what you believe and this is what we believe," pointing at the piece of paper with that week's Scripture verses printed on it. "We cannot force this upon you," we said. We reassured our friends that we would continue to love them and carry a friendship, but we would focus our time on searching for others who were more open to the message. We had come to the realization that it was indeed time to move on — like Jesus instructed us to do in Luke 6.

However, it seemed that Silas was not amused with the fact we were not willing to argue and only heightened his tone and shame of the Bible. He looked at that week's Scripture verse on the page and noticed that one particular verse stated that Jesus was the Son of God. He looked at each of us in the eye and said, "I do not believe!" as he took a pen and physically marked out the words.

His game did not work, but the meeting did end in a downcast way. The downward cycle of discouragement only continued, now turning into frustration. We kept wishing we could change the heart of every man in that room. We lamented in prayer fervently for these men's souls, asking God to make himself known to them, to pursue them boldly! And I can tell you, today, that God is faithful and does answer prayers.

A few weeks later, we noticed that Russell, the man we originally labeled a person of peace, was continuing to seek us out and ask questions. So, we continued to share in one-on-one meetings, using the 3/3 format mixed with testimonies. As we continued to share and study, we noticed Russell was growing in receptivity and even stated that he was having dreams of Jesus and feeling God stir in his heart. A breakthrough was beginning to take place.

One night, my teammates and I were having dinner when we received a text from Russell that stated, "We were talking about you guys, my friends. We really want to change. That's what we [have decided] to do. This relationship is so powerful and [I] am so sure it's from God." In excitement, we race to Russell's place of residence to discuss next steps and to see who aside from Russell was present.

Upon arrival at Russell's residence, I walked in the room and remember seeing three young men. One being Russell and his best friend with whom he had been sharing the stories of Jesus from our 3/3 meetings, but also a man that I would have never expected. Silas sat next to Russel, with a sobered look masking his face. Before I could say a word, Silas looked at me and said, "My friend, I must first apologize to you. Ever since that day I marked out those words, I went to my room and I have since experienced something that I cannot explain. I feel something right here, as he pointed to his heart, and I must say - I believe. What you say is true, and I believe!" (paraphrasing) A few days later, Russell, along with his best friend, and also Silas were all baptized. We gave praise to God for the growth in our friends and in His Kingdom. It was as if we were stepping into the days of Acts, seeing God powerfully move and add to our numbers. My desire is for all to see similar mighty works of God's hand, and I tell you, you can. A 3/3 group will not look uniform and will never work as perfectly as you might have imagined while you were going through the training, but I can say today that this model does work. Is it difficult? Yes. Will there be opposition? Yes. However, this model has a central mission of relying on the power of the Holy Spirit and sharing with others. Without these things, progress does not take place, and movements do not ensue. If someone who was so opposed to the Bible was, in turn, changed by this and, most importantly, is now making disciples, I'm convinced it works. Why? Because God works through it for He is the only who can change hearts! God taught me a lot in those particular weeks. That being, we are in partnership with Him as we make disciples, and this model goes nowhere if we do not involve Him in the process.

May God grant you the resilience and determination to fight the battle with the evil one. May His mighty power be strong within you.

Photo 42: May God grant you resilience.

Questions for Discussion:

1. This chapter presents 17 tools or tips for those wishing to launch CPM/DMM in their particular context. Pick out the top three approaches that would seem the most practical and effective for you, in your church or context. Explain why you chose those three.

2. Consider the idea of making a list of people for whom you will pray. Does it bother you to think you might be on such a list (that someone else made)? Explain why or why not.

3. For your learning style and preferences, would you rather learn "Creation to Judgment" (C2J) or the Three Circles Life Conversation? Explain why. What would it take for you to learn such a tool well? Would it be helpful? If so, what's stopping you?

4. This chapter mentioned that it might feel, at first, intimidating to think of baptizing someone. Does it seem that way to you? Why or why not?

5. Is it hard for you to lead others? (For example, are you afraid you're not good enough to do so?) Explain your answer by referencing the section, "Duckling Discipleship."

CHAPTER 13

FREQUENTLY ASKED QUESTIONS

Who is leading the charge in understanding CPM/DMM today?

In Chapter 2, we mentioned the coalition, 24:14. They would never presume to say they are "leading the charge," but they do represent a wide swath of implementers who are seeing God work mightily in their midst. The coalition came to fruition following two international summits which brought together leaders from organizations, churches, networks, and movements that were already committed to reaching the unreached through CPMs/DMMs from around the world. At those summits, they began with the question: "What will it take or cost to pray and work together to start kingdom movements in every unreached people and place in our generation?" (24:14, 2018) The question acted as a lightning rod for partnership. The Holy Spirit moved 24:14 Summit attendees to humbly pursue a unified effort to reach the unreached specifically through church planting movements (CPMs) with urgency by 2025. 24:14 has brought together leaders from organizations like Beyond, East West, Ethne, e3 Partners, the Antioch Movement, Latin Link, the IMB, Transformational Disciple Making Ministries, Frontiers, Global Assistance Partners, Austin Stone Community Church, the Global Alliance for Church Multiplication, All Nations Family, Lifeway Mission International, New Generations, Launch Global, Team Expansion and Zúme Project, along with others too sensitive to name.

24:14 is not an organization. As mentioned above, it is a coalition of like-minded individuals, practitioners and organizations who have made a commitment to a vision (to engage every unreached people and place with an effective kingdom movement strategy by December 31, 2025) based on four values:

1. Reaching the unreached in line with Matthew 24:14, that is, to bring the gospel of the kingdom to every unreached people and place.
2. Accomplishing this through "church planting movements," involving multiplying disciples, churches, leaders, and movements themselves.
3. Having a wartime sense of urgency to engage every unreached people and place with a movement strategy by the end of 2025.
4. Doing these things in collaboration with others.

The Dec. 31, 2025 goal isn't specifying fruit. It's describing engagement. They want a team (local or expatriate or combination) equipped in movement strategy to be on location in every unreached people and place by that date. They're not saying there will be a movement going on there. (See https://www.2414now.net/faqs.)

There have been plans and campaigns like these before. What makes this one any different, you might ask? William O'Brien and Keith Parks set out to answer that very question in their article in *Mission Frontiers* in January, 2018, entitled, in fact, "Why is 24:14 Different than Previous Efforts?" (O'Brien & Parks, 2018) They offer several reasons that 24:14 is different, with one of the key reasons being that, "effective CPM engagement that can result in the multiplication of disciples necessary to see an unreached group truly reached." As a result, we humbly point to 24:14 suggesting that it might be a movement we all ought to watch.

How does CPM/DMM view existing churches?

The church is the bride of Christ (Eph. 5:23). Jesus gave Himself to save it. He loves it. He loves us. Those who advocate for CPM/DMM strategies and life practices are often seen as recommending an improvement to the typical posture of the modern-day congregation.

These kinds of comments are never meant to take anything away from God's church. CPM/DMM trainers never want to trash the bride of Christ — nor should they. (Nor should any of us.) Many of our comments in this book refer to a "simple church." This is never meant to take away from a larger "regional" or "city" church. We praise the Lord for "regional" and "city" churches which have stood firm as long-term lighthouses of the gospel in neighborhoods and nations. However, our proposals in this book would hold that, in addition to these large-scale gatherings, there is good, biblical evidence that a smaller, group-oriented "simple church" might be good for us as disciples. In addition, most churches in the New Testament seem to be groups that were meeting in someone's house or beside a river. They were "simple churches." So please understand - we are FOR regional and city churches. Most of our advocacy in this book is for what's missing: **the simple church.** So in cases of regional or city churches, we believe they would be greatly strengthened by the presence of dozens (or hundreds) of "simple churches" within the larger body. They become "simple churches" within the realm of larger "regional" or "city" churches. That seems to be the situation in the New Testament — and that's what we're advocating for today as well.

Does CPM/DMM focus on making disciples or starting churches?

Yes.

In the Bible, we are commanded to do both. For example, in Matthew 28:19-20, Jesus doesn't say we should start churches. He instructs us to "make disciples." Yet the apostle Paul clearly reminded Titus 1:5, "The reason I left you in Crete was that you might put in order what was left unfinished and appoint elders in every town, as I directed you."

That sounds like a very specific, church-centric mission. Jesus tells Peter, "And I tell you that you are Peter, and on this rock I will build my church, and the gates of Hades will not overcome it" (Matthew 16:18). Yet Paul spells out the strategy in 2 Timothy 2:2, "And the things you have heard me say in the presence of many witnesses entrust to reliable people who will also be qualified to teach others." So the truth is, making disciples and church multiplication go hand in hand. In fact, a careful reading of Acts 14:21-28 causes one to wonder if Luke is perhaps using the words interchangeably:

Photo 43: The Bible commands us both to make disciples and form churches.

> They preached the gospel in that city and won a large number of disciples. Then they returned to Lystra, Iconium and Antioch, strengthening the disciples and encouraging them to remain true to the faith. "We must go through many hardships to enter the kingdom of God," they said. Paul and Barnabas appointed elders for them in each church and, with prayer and fasting, committed them to the Lord, in whom they had put their trust. After going through Pisidia, they came into Pamphylia, and when they had preached the word in Perga, they went down to Attalia.
>
> From Attalia they sailed back to Antioch, where they had been committed to the grace of God for the work they had now completed. On arriving there, they gathered the church together and reported all that God had done through them and how he had opened a door of faith to the Gentiles. And they stayed there a long time with the disciples.

Luke is essentially using the word church as a synonym for disciples (Bosch, 2001).

Is CPM/DMM focused mainly on tactics?

Some have misunderstood the nature of CPM/DMM. They have somehow been duped to think that CPM/DMM is a magic wand. Wave this wand in this way and a movement will result. Unfortunately, such is not the case. CPM/DMM is a set of principles, strategies, life practices, and behaviors. When practiced in biblical ways, they significantly remove obstacles from blocking the flow of God's Spirit to bring about change and redemption. It's as simple as that. Become a disciple worth multiplying and — bam – you increase the likelihood exponentially that God can use you to make other disciples.

Does CPM/DMM always happen to groups?

Somewhere along the line, some CPM/DMM trainers insisted that we should only win groups to Christ, entire families at a time. Unfortunately, there are instances in the New Testament in which God helped His people win just ONE person at a time too. Therefore, we know (factually) that the task of reaching villages and people groups is non-sequential. Is it **BETTER** that an entire relational network convert to Christ at once? Sure. Does it always have to happen that way? Of course not. We know this because we've seen it as biblical fact. (For example, the Ethiopian Treasurer, Acts 8.) Please don't let the good of CPM/DMM be lumped together with the misunderstanding that the gospel can only flow to groups.

How does CPM/DMM impact people group thinking?

Since the beginning of "people group thinking" (somewhere around International Congress on World Evangelization in Lausanne, Switzerland in 1974 (Lausanne Movement, 2018)) mission educators and strategists began helping organizations and churches to think about the world as a tapestry of "people groups," rather than merely as a list of political nations. For evangelization purposes, a people group is usually defined as "the largest group within which the gospel can spread as a church planting movement without encountering barriers of understanding or acceptance" (Billy Graham Center, 2018). An unreached people group is a people group among which there is no indigenous community of believing Christians with adequate numbers and resources to evangelize this people group without outside assistance. One of the leading providers of data about unreached people groups is Joshua Project. (By the way, Joshua Project uses the terms "unreached" and "least-reached" to mean the same thing.) In trying to establish a benchmark for listing unreached people groups objectively, the original Joshua Project editorial committee selected the criteria less than or equal to 2% Evangelical Christian and less than or equal to 5% Professing Christians. These benchmarks are designed to provide guidance for those designing strategies and mobilizing God's people for action.

It's important to understand that, in many locations, these people groups intermingle, mixing in the very same territories, cities, and villages. As a result, mission strategists and mobilizers have realized over the years that, when defining goals and designing strategies, it is actually **most** helpful to look at both peoples **and** places. When it comes to reaching the world, an effective mission strategy should enter a new territory, village or city with "people group

Photo 44: We must approach each new situation with people group eyes and see where the church isn't.

eyes," keeping in mind the natural limitations of political

districts and other externally-imposed boundaries. When comparing the relative value of people groups and places, It's never "either/or;" it's "both/and."

Isn't CPM/DMM focused too much on "works?"

Because CPM/DMM talks a lot about obedience-based discipleship, some mistakenly believe it is **all** about works. It's not. It's about prayer. It's about faith. It's about listening to God. It's about nurturing the Spirit. Do we dumb-down Christianity and say, "Shall we go on sinning so that grace may increase" (Romans 6:1)? God forbid. Jesus commanded us to teach them to obey everything that He had commanded them to do. So that's what we try to do. Jesus said we would be known by our fruit (visible acts of obedience as evidence in our lives — Matthew 7:15-20). He also taught that it would be obvious whether or not we know Him by the way we keep his commands (John 2:3). James said faith without works is dead (James 2:17). Obedience flows out of gratitude for God's mercy (Romans 12:1). Even as Paul viewed God's mercy, it prompted him to live like a human sacrifice. Paul's view of obedience was strong. He wrote, "Circumcision is nothing and uncircumcision is nothing. Keeping God's commands is what counts" (1 Corinthians 7:19). So the apostle to the Gentiles, who advocated a life built in grace and free from works, still wrote that "keeping God's commands is what counts."

So, bottom line, our obedience to God isn't forced as a "work." Just because CPM/DMM builds an accountability process into the system, it isn't taking Christianity back to a yoke of Judaism. Exactly the opposite is true. Jesus replied, "Anyone who loves me will obey my teaching. My Father will love them, and we will come to them and make our home with them" (John 14:23). Obedience is God's selected favorite path to show Him our love for Him and through which He reveals even more of Himself to us.

Do CPM/DMM practitioners believe only in "discipling people to faith" or discipling only "Persons of Peace?"

Some CPM/DMM implementers have pointed out that not everyone in a 3/3 group has to be a believer already. Some can come to Christ within a 3/3 group as they study the Word. Some implementers have pointed out that a 3/3 group could even conceivably be led by a non-Christian. Those instances have happened. They have actually taken place. However, CPM/DMM implementers would never insist that this is the only way people can come to faith. Sometimes, a person will accept Jesus upon hearing a believer's testimony. Sometimes, non-Christians will accept Christ when they hear a presentation of the full, clear gospel message — say, the story of "Creation to Judgment" (C2J as it's sometimes called). Other times, non-Christians come to faith within the context of a 3/3 group. All of these instances have happened and they're all good.

Likewise, some have emphasized that outsiders should only disciple "Persons of Peace." However, it's important to understand that, in working with CPM/DMM approaches, life isn't always tidy and organized. What's more, no one is wearing a name badge with a label on it, clearly identifying that person as a "person of peace." What we're trying to say is, these movements are fluid; we have to be flexible and follow God's Spirit in implementing them. There are indeed over all "best practices," but at the end of the day, it is God who births and leads a CPM/DMM, not man.

Do we find in the New Testament any examples of 3/3 groups?

Well, discovery Bible studies are missing from the New Testament. Consequently, the truth is, most people (99%?) didn't have access to Scripture — period. (The New Testament wasn't even assembled yet, obviously.) Besides, arguments from silence are the weakest arguments of all. (They didn't use DVD Bible studies in the New Testament either.)

Was there ever a biblical instance of a non-believer leading someone to the Lord?

Yes. The woman at the well (John 4).

Do all CPM/DMM practitioners do things exactly alike?

Unfortunately, there's no one copyrighted line on CPM/DMM. No one person "invented it." Criticizing "CPM/DMM" is about like criticizing a group of Bible teachers from all over the world. Everybody teaches a little bit differently.

Is CPM/DMM the only way for the Kingdom to grow?

Definitely not. Many of us (most of us?) came to Christ through other expressions of the church. CPM/DMM is working well in many contexts. It's not working as well in others. No matter what, we celebrate it when the work of the Lord goes forward.

Do CPM/DMM practitioners believe CPM/DMM is the only way?

In a word, no. There are many ways people can be brought closer to Christ. However, there is no doubt that God is working through CPM/DMM approaches to bring many people into His Kingdom. As a result, we believe it should not be overlooked or kicked out of the toolbox.

Is CPM/DMM a fad?

Some fear that disciple-making movement practices will come and go like the latest fad, like hula-hoops or bell-bottom trousers. Faithful trainers point to multiple Scripture passages (like 2 Tim. 2:2) which describe timeless principles and heartfelt daily disciplines. These trainers would rather view CPM/DMM practices as if we are finally getting something right. Even if CPM/DMM is a fad, it seems to be an effective one for the time being. David Garrison has written in *A Wind in the House of Islam* (p. 18), after examining a voluminous amount of research and conducting first-hand interviews literally around the world, "in Islam's first 12 centuries we found no voluntary and only a handful of coerced, conversions to the Christian religion." He adds that "By the close of the 20th century, ... there had been a total of 13 movements of Muslim communities to faith in Jesus Christ." Garrison is defining a movement of Christ as consisting of at least 1000 baptisms. He adds, "In only the first 12 years of the 21st century, an additional 69 movements to Christ" have taken place. Since the writing of his book, all movements worldwide now total 651 (Trousdale, 2018, p. 34). So if it's a fad, please pray with us that we can make it last as long as possible. And if it's not, then the church might as well get on board sooner rather than later.

How does CPM/DMM impact those working in urban contexts?

It's no secret that the world is becoming a city. The United Nations has gone on record saying that, as of the end of 2017, some 55% of the world is urban. One writer at Devex has gone on record saying that researchers at the European Commission have now used high resolution satellite imagery to show that an estimated 84% of us now live in cities (Cheney, 2018). It probably depends more on words and definitions, but either way, urban sprawls are a complex place to live.

Photo 45: 55% of the world is now urban.

What's more, living in cities is expensive. This places tremendous stress on those seeking to start traditional churches. Trousdale addresses this in *The Kingdom Unleashed*. He writes,

"The traditional Global North paradigm costs so much because most of our funds are spent on buildings, staff, and programs that don't make replicating disciples. It is obvious that we need to look for biblically grounded paradigms that are proven to work" (p. 270).

The good news is that CPM/DMM approaches have shown to be effective in both rural areas and urban areas alike. One would never be advised to reduce Kingdom outreach to mere dollars-and-cents considerations. Having said that, we'd be crazy not to point out that the simplicity of CPM/DMM strategies make a lot of sense to those who are trying to stretch today's mission dollars to the max.

How can we minimize or avert Heresy?

The great thing about CPM/DMM is that the Bible is used as the highest authority. Scripture is held higher than the opinions of humankind. The coalition, 24:14, has emphasized this as well, explaining that

> heresy is generally less prevalent in movements because of the very interactive nature of discipleship. Heresy is a seed the enemy sows among groups of believers whether they are a part of movements or traditional churches. The question is not whether the enemy will sow such problems but whether we are equipping disciples and churches to guard against false teachings and address them when they arise. Even the New Testament church faced such challenges, but equipping believers to rely on Scripture as their authority and study the Scripture together as the body (as in Acts 17:11) helps guard against creative and eloquent false teachers. A focus on obedience-based discipleship instead of knowledge-based discipleship also protects against heresy. In other words, disciples are not just committed to gaining knowledge, but the measure of their discipleship is obedience to that knowledge (24:14, 2018).

How can we keep a movement solid long-term?

This question has come up again and again. One of the best answers comes from Scott Ridout, who was featured at the 2018 GACX conference (Ridout, 2018). He proposed that we constantly ask nine questions to maximize the possibility that a movement will keep expanding. Those nine questions are:

1. Are the Leaders Spiritually Vibrant?
2. Is the Vision Clear and Compelling?
3. Is the Theology sound?
4. Are systems/methods effective?
5. Are the steps simple?
6. Are the Relationships strong?
7. Are the influencers/leaders engaged?
8. Are the Benefits clear and communicated?
9. Is progress/impact celebrated?

Obviously, sustaining a movement involves many facets. These questions should at least get the discussion rolling.

Is CPM/DMM for everyone?

In a word, yes. Jesus told his closest followers, in Matthew 28:19-20 to "Make disciples of all nations." Then, a few breaths later, he told them to train those new disciples to "do everything he had commanded **them** (his closest followers) to do." In other words, the command to make disciples is a repeating chain. It was supposed to go viral. But what does that mean? And how would it happen?

The first (and the core) level of what Jesus was commanding was to "make disciples." Becoming a disciple means becoming like Jesus. Courses like Zúme, along with many of the live trainings mentioned in this book, are designed to be like a "Christian 101" class. They are designed to answer the question, "How do we become like Jesus?" For this reason, these courses (including Zúme) are indeed for everyone. Every believer needs to be a person of the Word, prayer, body life, and able to respond well to persecution. Every believer needs to hear from Him, because those who don't **hear** from Him don't have any part of Him. Jesus said, "Whoever belongs to God hears what God says. The reason you do not hear is that you do not belong to God" (John 8:47). Being a disciple of Jesus is more about being like Jesus than attending any particular course or training. These trainings and this Zúme course just give us a handy template that makes the training more transferable... more reproducible. They help us remember concepts and how to present them. Being like Jesus means doing what He did.

Some people misunderstand these trainings. They believe CPM/DMM is just for some people. In those cases, they are likely viewing CPM/DMM as a method, a program, a fad, or a particular strategy — and not as a lifestyle of obediently following Jesus the way He told us to.

As far as the Great Commission goes, clearly we're all supposed to be involved in its fulfillment, in one way or another. However, it goes without saying that our roles might vary. Take, for example, a church which is considering a capital campaign to raise funds for a new worship center. The leadership of the church might choose to utilize a tag-line that reads, "We can't all give equal gifts; but we can all make an equal sacrifice." In the context of a capital campaign, we accept the fact that some people in the church are blessed with extra funds. Perhaps they inherited a farm or a fortune from parents or grandparents. Maybe they discovered mineral deposits under their farm and sold the mining-rights. Or maybe they were blessed with entrepreneurial skills. Maybe they started a chain of fast-food restaurants that has now paid them back handsomely for all the time, energy, and effort they invested in the start-up. When it comes time to fill out commitment cards, the spokesperson for the campaign will ask everyone to make an equal sacrifice. For the college student with lots of student loans and only a part-time job delivering pizzas, that equal sacrifice might be a relatively small gift. For the retiring President/CEO of that fast-food business, it might be a very large

Photo 46: We don't all have equal gifts, but we can all be involved in the effort of making disciples in some way.

gift. The leadership is asking everyone in the church to participate with equal sacrifice. The gifts themselves are different. The mobilization cry of equal sacrifice helps everyone feel equally involved and, if implemented well, the church might well reach its stretch goal for the new worship center.

Another perspective: In wartime, we've often heard that for every person on the front lines, there are six people behind the lines who are providing infrastructure and support, building weapons, rolling bandages, cooking meals, etc. The important thing to realize is that every single person needs to know **how** to implement, even if not everyone always is in the driver's seat with a stranger. Curtis Sergeant has addressed this topic well with his talk, "Every marine a rifleman" (Sergeant, Multiplication Concepts, 2018). He points out that, in the U.S. Marines, even if a person is going to be an administrative assistant, he or she still goes to Basic Training and still learns to shoot a rifle. Because Marines have a stated value that "every Marine is a rifleman." Likewise, it appears that Jesus wants every Christian to be a part of making disciples.

CPM/DMM is like that. The word, "evangelism," means sharing the good news of Jesus Christ with another person. It could be as simple as Andrew going to seek Peter, his brother. He told Peter, "We have found the Messiah" (John 1:41). It could also be Paul and his colleagues intentionally seeking out a place of prayer on the Sabbath (Acts 16:11-15). A businesswoman named Lydia had been trying to worship God, but apparently didn't understand the story of Jesus. Once Paul explained it, she captured it in full and gave her life to Christ. Later in the same chapter (verse 40), when Paul and his team were released from jail, they went to Lydia's house. She apparently had gathered a home Bible study there. (She was already at work sharing her new-found faith.) Paul and others encouraged Lydia's friends then departed. Evangelism, as they say, is like "one beggar telling another where to find bread." This kind of evangelism is a privilege and responsibility for every believer, regardless of our personality or gifts. **We can all tell the story of our changed lives.**

The Bible also speaks of a specific **gift** of evangelism, however. See for example, Ephesians 4:11-13. Paul wrote, "So Christ himself gave the apostles, the prophets, the evangelists, the pastors and teachers, to equip his people for works of service, so that the body of Christ may be built up until we all reach unity in the faith and in the knowledge of the Son of God and become mature, attaining to the whole measure of the fullness of Christ." We don't have a clear definition of this gift, but presumably we can observe it in the lives of great men and women of God like Paul, Peter, and even modern-day followers like Billy Graham. They are somehow able to speak to large groups and change hearts in an unfathomable way. The early Church faced rapid growth, at times.

> In those days when the number of disciples was increasing, the Hellenistic Jews among them complained against the Hebraic Jews because their widows were being overlooked in the daily distribution of food. So the Twelve gathered all the disciples together and said, "It would not be right for us to neglect the ministry of the word of God in order to wait on tables. Brothers and sisters, choose seven men from among you who are known to be full of the Spirit and wisdom. We will turn this responsibility over to them and will give our attention to prayer and the ministry of the word.
>
> This proposal pleased the whole group. They chose Stephen, a man full of faith and of the Holy Spirit; also Philip, Procorus, Nicanor, Timon, Parmenas, and Nicolas from Antioch, a convert to Judaism. They presented these men to the apostles, who prayed and laid their hands on them.
>
> So the word of God spread. The number of disciples in Jerusalem increased rapidly, and a large number of priests became obedient to the faith (Acts 6:1-7).

In this passage, the leaders of the early Church appointed servants to deal with distributing food so the apostles could focus on their task and gift of ministering the word. They chose proven, good Christian people and made it clear that serving food to the poor was important too. It was such an important gift, the leaders laid hands on them and prayed to set them apart. As a result, God blessed the church with even **more** growth. Now one could argue that, just because these servants were helping distribute food, it didn't mean they weren't telling the good news to others. (In fact, we know they did just that. Philip is called to tell the Ethiopian treasurer about the Good News just two chapters later in Acts 8.) However, it **does** mean there are times that we might be called upon to serve the church in other special ways. If and when that happens, we should never feel somehow like we are less valuable, nor should we cause others to feel less valuable either. Not every believer has the same gift, but we are all called upon to be involved in the growth of the church.

Photo 47: Some might have the gift of evangelism. But somehow, we all need to be involved in the overall effort of making disciples.

Those who have a gift to play a certain sport are often unable to understand why others can't play it. That doesn't mean we can't all enjoy a good pickup soccer game. Just because we aren't super-apostles, it doesn't mean we can't tell our brother about the Messiah. All of us who have discovered the Messiah are privileged and obligated to share with those around us. In fact, Matthew 28 **compels** us to care about reaching the whole world. Somehow, we have to be involved in finishing the task. We are driven by the love and grace we have each received. Christ's love compels us.

Those who have the **gift** of evangelism had better do all the more to spread His fame.

Questions for Discussion:

1. This chapter attempts to discuss how CPM/DMM views the existing church. Explain why that question is difficult to answer. (Hint: Remember that "CPM/DMM" isn't an organization but an organic collection of strategies and life practices.) In light of what you've now learned (or learned previously) about CPM/DMM, how do you view the existing church. (Remember -- never trash the bride of Christ.) In an ideal world, what would be your perfect design for the church?

2. Sometimes in the past, the idea of "discipleship" has meant other things than the way the term "disciple-making" is being used in CPM/DMM world. Compare and contrast with some of the meanings you've heard previously. How is the CPM/DMM usage helpful or not helpful? Why?

3. This chapter pointed out that some CPM/DMM trainers emphasize only baptizing groups (never individuals). How do you feel about this idea? This chapter asserted that the Bible gave examples of instances in which individuals were allowed to come to Christ as individuals. Do you agree or disagree? How do you reconcile these two seeming contradictions between some trainers' philosophy and these case studies from the Bible?

4. Analyze the difference between emphasizing "works" and accountability (in CPM/DMM strategies). How do you feel about the difference?

5. Do you think CPM/DMM will, in the end, be a fad? Give your reasoning.

CHAPTER 14

A CALL FOR UNITY

In some ways, it's rather astonishing that the majority of these church-planting movements are so similar in nature. We use the word astonishing, because no one has tried to copyright, trademark, or even claim credit for these practices. Though we highlighted several key books in Chapter 2, these practices didn't really originate with the publication of any one landmark "how-to" manual or guidebook. David Garrison, Steve Smith, Curtis Sergeant, Ying Kai, David Watson, Jerry Trousdale, Bruce Carlton, Kent Parks, Bill Smith and others have written and trained about their experiences with movements toward Christ, but, though their opinions vary on certain practices, no one trainer has claimed to have absolute truth on the subject. In fact, to the contrary, many of these trainers almost deflect the attention that CPM/DMM outcomes have given them. They constantly remind us of the fact that these appear to be movements of God. Most trainers avoid referring to these strategies as a curriculum, preferring instead to view these practices as a kind of lifestyle or a biblical approach to life. So perhaps CPM/DMM practices might best be viewed as a series of streams that have, over the past two decades, merged into a powerful set of rivers, all of which are surging with power, but none of which is claiming to be a "sole revelation from God." We say "rivers" (plural) because these trainers are likely not united on each and every teaching. Still, the practices don't vary that much. Some have ventured an estimate that practitioners and trainers vary in their teachings on as little as 10% of their practices. Most trainers are, in fact, incredibly consistent, as if God is the one behind them all. It's actually quite remarkable.

At the same time, if there are differences, what **are** some examples? We'll mention a few that we've observed.

For example, some trainers believe that, when looking for Persons of Peace, one should be quite bold — almost the way an evangelist would go door-to-door with the gospel message. Now to be fair, they really aren't advocating going door-to-door, but it might **seem** that way to their counterparts in the CPM/DMM world, who feel that the proper approach is to be much more culturally sensitive, as they would say. So the "bold" kind of CPM/DMM practitioner would, for example, do prayer walking along a downtown street, asking a person on a park bench if there's anything for which he or she could pray. By doing so, the CPM/DMM practitioner is "filtering" for someone who is interested in prayer and in spiritual conversations. By contrast, the more "laid back" CPM/DMM implementer might be appalled at such a practice. He or she might rather say to the person on the park bench, "Nice weather God is making today." This "shemah" statement might be ignored by someone who isn't spiritually inclined. But the spiritually-minded person of peace will take note and, when the time is right, ask for more information about spiritual things. So the "bold" type of implementer is more proactive, while the "shemah" approach is a bit more reactive. "Bold" implementers refer to Scriptures like the Great Commission in Matt. 28:19-20, pointing out (accurately so) that Jesus's instruction to make disciples is in the imperative mode. It's a command. It's active. But the more passive witness might argue that, in today's secular climate, we risk offending people if we "push our beliefs into their faces." Either way, you, the implementer, will have to decide which route you take. In this book, we teach the more active, bold approach. But you can decide how your approach will look. Maybe Simon Peter was more outgoing, and maybe Andrew didn't speak as much, but Jesus wanted both of them to be part of the 12. The important thing is that they both need to be engaged in making disciples, somehow.

Another example — some trainers have developed a line of thinking that emphasizes working with and winning **groups** at all costs, at every level. This often has deep implications at the family level. If the wife wants to accept Christ, some implementers will often seek to delay her, hoping to win the husband at the same time. These implementers point out that, to do it any other way is to split families. The same thing might be said of homogenous villagers. Group-oriented implementers believe so strongly that if one doesn't wait for the whole village, one will always ultimately lose any stragglers who might come to Christ alone, anyway. By contrast, there's another strain of CPM/DMM strategy that basically says, "Hey, a soul is a soul. If only one member of the family accepts Christ as Lord, at least THAT member will have now escaped Hell — and can begin trying to win her friends, even if her family doesn't respond." Of course, in cultures known to be group-oriented, multi-individual, mutually-interdependent "people movement" decisions are huge (just ask Donald McGavran). So, truth be known, there are lots of extenuating circumstances in making these decisions. But, more often than not, the group-oriented CPM/DMM implementers will shy away from implementers who are willing to receive "the one" into the fold.

They just fear that it is "poison in the well."

So what we're trying to say here is that there is a bit of a spectrum — across that last 10% of CPM/DMM practices. Some even make a huge deal about what to call these practices (whether to call them CPM, SCMM, T4T, or

Photo 48: Let's all be ONE so that the world can be WON.

whatever). If there's one conclusion we'd like to propose here, it's that, there are so few people practicing CPM/DMM so far... so few churches incorporating the strategy into their plans and so few missionaries implementing these practices as of yet, we don't believe we can afford the luxury of arguing about the last 10%. We should celebrate ANY and ALL engagement with CPM/DMM principles. And biblically speaking there are arguments on both sides. There are plenty of times biblical figures focused on winning entire households (like the Philippian jailer's family in Acts 16). But there are also instances in which a biblical figure addressed a solo character (like the Ethiopian treasurer in Acts 8). Because there are arguments on both sides, we figure we should follow the Spirit's leading and do both, reaching out to both individuals **and** groups.

This brings us to our important conclusion: In this and all things, let's remember that Jesus prayed, in John 17, that we would all be one so that the world would be WON. Please — in this entire area of strategies and approaches, please try to avoid dissensions. Paul wrote, in 1 Corinthians 1:10-13:

> I appeal to you, brothers and sisters, in the name of our Lord Jesus Christ, that all of you agree with one another in what you say and that there be no divisions among you, but that you be perfectly united in mind and thought. My brothers and sisters, some from Chloe's household have informed me that there are quarrels among you. What I mean is this: One of you says, "I follow Paul"; another, "I follow Apollos"; another, "I follow Cephas"; still another, "I follow Christ."
>
> Is Christ divided? Was Paul crucified for you? Were you baptized in the name of Paul?

So please... let's not say, "I follow David Watson," or "I follow Jerry Trousdale." Let's ALL say, instead, "I follow Christ."

Questions for Discussion:

1. Try to think of an example of a new product or movement that began with one individual or one company. In those cases, how did it help or hurt the promotion and acceptance of that product or movement? In your opinion, how does it help or hurt that CPM/DMM strategy wasn't "invented" or isn't shepherded, as such, by any one person or organization?

2. At this point in your understanding of implementing CPM/DMM strategy and life practices, would you rather be bold in your proclamation? ... or do you see yourself more "laid back?" How will you react when you meet someone who feels it's imperative to be more forthright in one's presentation of the Good News? Explain why.

3. Can you think of any other examples in which Godly men and women have disagreed about doctrine or biblical approaches? Name a couple and give examples of how this has helped or hurt the growth in Kingdom of God worldwide.

CHAPTER 15

EPILOGUE: UNDERSTANDING FAITHFULNESS

(Adapted with permission from a recording by Curtis Sergeant)

Did you ever consider that **faithfulness** is a much better measure of spiritual maturity than knowledge and training?

Orthodoxy vs. Orthopraxy

There are two ideas that have caused a number of problems in the church today.

The first is the idea that someone's spiritual maturity is connected to how much they know about God's Word. They act as if **right belief** - or orthodoxy - is a good measure of someone's faith. The problem with this idea is that Satan knows more Scripture than any human. **God's Word** says, "You believe that there is one God. Good! Even the demons believe that — and shudder" (James 2:19). A better measure of someone's spiritual maturity is **orthopraxy** - "right practice". We should be much more concerned with **faithfulness** in **obeying** and **sharing** than measuring maturity based only on what we know.

The second is the idea that someone's ability to lead requires a "full training" before they begin in ministry. He acts as if **complete knowledge** is a good measure of someone's ability to serve. The problem with this idea is that **no** one is ever really fully trained. Jesus modeled sending out young leaders. He would send people out to do some of the most important work in the Kingdom in spite of the fact that they might have very little formal training. God's Word says, "When Jesus had called the Twelve together, he gave them power and authority to drive out all demons and to cure diseases, and he sent them out to proclaim the kingdom of God and to heal the sick" (Luke 9:1-2). These men were sent before Peter shared his belief that Jesus was Savior — something we'd consider a first step of faith. And even after being sent, Jesus rebuked Peter multiple times for mistakes (e.g., Mark 8:33) and Peter would still later deny Jesus (Luke 22:54-62). Other followers argued over who was the greatest and what role each would play in God's future Kingdom (Luke 9:46). They all still had a lot to learn, but Jesus put them to work sharing what they already knew. Faithfulness, more than knowledge, is something that can start as soon as someone begins to follow Jesus.

The big difference between these two patterns is that one delays significant implementation until people reach a certain level of maturity or expertise or knowledge. The other asks people to begin implementing – to begin using what they learn from the moment they enter the kingdom of God. This is a pretty stark contrast. Critics will point to the fact that a new believer might make some mistakes now and then. He or she might make an error in thinking, speaking, or even doing. Some critics will seize on this and insist that it shouldn't be tolerated, but for a child to learn to ride a bicycle they need to be able to get on the bicycle and as we've pointed out previously, we can never get to a point in which all believers reach perfection anyway. The good news

Photo 49: Sooner or later, we have to trust the learner to ride the bike solo.

is – using the life practices discussed throughout this book, new believers will grow fairly quickly. It's also highly likely that, in the meantime, any mistakes they make will not cause serious damage because the community of Christ will likely excuse them precisely because everyone will recognize that they're new to the faith. After all, Jesus sent out the disciples very shortly after having called them. He didn't even wait until he had been with them for his short three-year ministry. In fact, he sends them out fairly soon after meeting them (Luke 9). Based on Jesus's example, it shouldn't stop us from entrusting new disciples today either.

Lessons from Learning to Ride a Bike

This is very much parallel to a child learning to ride a bicycle. In order for a child to learn to ride a bicycle he/she needs to be able to get on the bicycle and probably to fall down a few times before he has enough expertise to be able to ride proficiently. There is no way around this. People need to get on the bicycle and be allowed to fall before they learn to ride well. Wanting more advanced training before putting them on the bike is equivalent to asking someone to sit on a couch and watch the Tour de France bicycle race for three weeks and then taking them out, giving them a bicycle, and expecting them to know how to ride. They still don't know how to ride. No matter how good the modeling was, no matter how proficient their examples and teachers were, they still have to learn to get on the bike and ride, and they will still make mistakes. Professional bicycle riders fall down. One never actually reaches the point of perfection in bike-riding.

We have to become more accepting and more forgiving of mistakes, especially early on in someone's development. We have to realize that God will get over it. One would think that, at least here in the United States, people who have been using these approaches for many years would be producing outstanding disciples; but it's simply not the case. We focus heavily on knowledge, and we emphasize the importance of orthodoxy. This is wonderful. Orthodoxy is important; however, Satan is orthodox. Satan knows more Scripture than any follower of Christ, but he does not respond appropriately to what he knows. Instead, he resists the Lord. Orthodoxy in and of itself is meaningless.

We tend to use knowledge as a measure of maturity when really there is no such thing. Maturity takes time, and there is no way a new believer can be totally mature in his faith. We spend too much time focusing on maturity. Instead, we should focus on faithfulness. I believe faithfulness can be measured best by the ratio of how much someone knows to how much they obey and apply. I believe we should be focusing on how much they pass on to others what they have learned. These three aspects are like three legs of a stool. A stool is not usable unless the three legs are equal length. The disciple is not faithful unless these three legs are equal length: knowledge, application, and sharing (passing on to others). We see these concepts tied together throughout Scripture.

For example, Ezra is noted as being one who knew, obeyed, and taught the Word of the Lord (Ezra 7:10). There are many passages that tie these aspects together. In the heavenly economy, God invests more in those who are faithful with what they've already been given. A new believer can be absolutely faithful long before he or she is mature as long as he or she knows one thing, obeys it, and passes it on to others. This kind of disciple is being faithful, and this is the kind of person into whom God invests more. In fact, one might even go so far as to say that to give a new believer a tremendous amount of knowledge is counterproductive. It's like a rainstorm that brings rainfall far too quickly for the ground to absorb, and it results in flash floods. What is needed instead is a slow, steady rainfall that comes at a pace that can be absorbed by the ground. This is the type of training that needs to happen. It's not something that can happen in a big chunk because we are setting people up for failure. We know this to be true by looking at current surveys and population studies.

Survey Said...

Lifeway Research recently conducted a poll of 3000 evangelical believers throughout the USA (Smietana, 2016). It was amazing how mixed up Americans were in spite of the abundance of churches with their seminary-trained pastors preaching on practically every street corner in the USA.

- Six in 10 said everyone eventually goes to heaven.
- Two-thirds said they believed Jesus is God; but one out of every two who responded said Jesus is a being created by God.
- Two-thirds of Americans (64 percent) said God accepts the worship of all religions, including Christianity, Judaism, and Islam.
- Seventy-four percent of Americans disagreed with the idea that even the smallest sin deserves eternal damnation.
- Fewer than half of Americans (47 percent) said the Bible is 100 percent accurate in all it teaches.
- Six percent said the Holy Spirit is a force rather than a person.
- Forty-four percent said sex outside of traditional marriage is not a sin.
- Half of Americans (52%) said good deeds help them earn a spot in heaven.

All of the people who responded said they were evangelical Christians, but clearly they weren't reading the same Bible that you and I are reading. If our approaches to making disciples are so good, how did this situation become so bad? What's worse, according to researchers, is that the pastors of evangelical churches also have many unbiblical worldviews. In spite of this factor (and in spite of the fact that we know that these experts don't always have perfect knowledge), we still rely on clergy to instruct all God's people. The outcome is plain and simple: Not only do our church members sometimes receive faulty teaching, but in addition, the system continues to create a dependency and is not an effective way to make disciples. Disciples need to be taught how to feed themselves. This can happen only by a disciple applying what he or she learns and sharing it with others so that God chooses to invest more in him or her.

Scriptures Say...

There are plenty of examples in Scripture where people were thrust into ministry without long term training.

When Philip led the Ethiopian treasurer to faith (Acts 8:26-40) you will notice he didn't have any special training (as far as we know) in cross-cultural ministry. The moment the Ethiopian treasurer accepts Christ, he immediately goes out and, without further training, is now responsible for starting work in the nation of Ethiopia. There's no three-year seminary program (or even a 9-month internship) required before he goes out to share his faith.

The man with the impure spirit in Mark 5 is another example. Jesus casts the demons out of him. When the man wants to follow Jesus to learn more, Jesus says no (Mark 5:18-20). He sends him out immediately to share with his people the wonderful things that God had done for him. In all likelihood, this man was a Gentile, not a Jew, and he certainly didn't have any formal training. He didn't have a certificate from a special training school when this miracle occurred. This was Jesus's first time in that region as far as we know. When Jesus returns to this region some time later, He's met by great crowds of people who want Him to heal them or to cast out **their** demons (Mark 7:31-8:10). How did they know about Him? The likely answer is that the previ-ously-demon-possessed man spread the word. He was not

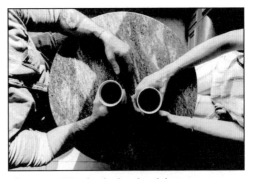

Photo 50: We think that by delaying someone, they'll become more ready. But perhaps we should release them for outreach the moment they convert.

required to go through a year-long training before sharing with others what God had done for him.

In the book of John there's a great example of how someone with no training or education can have legitimate spiritual insight even to a greater degree than those who have great training. The blind man was able to see who Jesus was while the Pharisees were not (John 9:1-34). The Pharisees still mocked the blind man. They said he could not know truth because he had not been trained. Yet, they were the ones who were blind. Their elitism that arose from their advanced training and study of Scripture blinded them to the truth. As Paul said, "There are not many wise, not many powerful" (1 Corinthians 1:26). No, God does not necessarily choose the things or people who are honored and respected in the world to be great in faith. It's a huge mistake to think that training is the key. **Faithfulness** is the key.

Education and training are good and they can be powerful tools but they are not a prerequisite. Formal training in theology and cross-cultural ministry do not guarantee good fruit. That's the type of system that produced the Pharisees. Jesus told the Pharisees, "You teach the precepts of men and ignore the commands of God" (Mark 7:7).

There are lots of examples of us doing this today.

- Jesus commands us to share our faith (Matthew 28:19-20). We tell new believers to wait until they're trained.
- Jesus commands people to be baptized when they believe (Mark 16:16. We tell people to wait until they complete a course and are trained and then they can be baptized.

These things that we're doing, we do from good motives, I believe. We want to preserve the purity of the church. We want to make sure that God's name is not dragged through the mud by people behaving badly. These are good things. Unfortunately that is not how God instructed us to deal with that issue. For example baptism is an initiation not a graduation. We want to make it into a graduation so that we can preserve the quality of the church. The way that God instructs us to preserve the purity of the church is by practicing church discipline but we do not want to practice church discipline. We find that uncomfortable so we find another way to accomplish that same purpose.

When someone comes to faith and immediately starts trying to apply and share, he or she might indeed make mistakes. But, again, that's like children learning to ride bicycles. That's natural and normal. We don't chide children for their efforts. We applaud their efforts and help them to do better. We don't say, "Oh I guess you're just not wired to ride a bicycle. So forget it." We continue to provide assistance and supervision as they continue to grow and improve until they get to the point in which they can ride the bicycle on their own. Then we help them continue to increase their ability until we know that they have all of the basic skills. They know how to get on the bicycle. If they fall off they can start on their own. They can steer, they can brake, and they can handle curves. They can handle hills and even combinations of all of these things. They know the rules of the road. They know when to ride and where to ride. We continue to actively coach them to help them grow. They have the full array of tools and we see that they are faithfully helping others to grow and developing in all of these areas. That process is not complete with a very initial training program. When new disciples apply and share what they're learning through CPM/DMM training, likewise, we should view it as normal. It's no different than a sophomore in a traditional Bible college being disciplined because he broke the rules and stayed out beyond curfew.

This idea of keeping knowledge, application, and teaching all at an even rate of development can be seen in passages like 2 Timothy 2:2. "And the things you have heard me say in the presence of many witnesses entrust to reliable people who will also be qualified to teach others."

We see it in the parable of the talents (Matthew 25:14-30). We see it in Matthew 10 where it says, "freely you have received freely give." We see it in Luke 12:48 where it says "from those to whom much has been given much shall be required." We have to trust the Holy Spirit in believers and His Word along with being responsible in our application of accountability within the body to be enough.

Jesus gives authority to every believer. When Jesus gave the Great Commission in Matthew 28, He told us to make disciples of all nations, and then He promised to be with us until the end of the age. The two go together. If we believe His promise (that He will be with us to the very end of the age) is to every follower of Christ then we must also acknowledge His command (to make disciples of all nations) is also to every disciple. Anything we do that prevents people from embarking upon a course to make disciples is a big mistake. If people understand that they are to do these things then they are to do them now, not when they can do them perfectly. They need to do these things now, not when someone else says they're ready to do it.

It's interesting that Jesus sent His disciples out early. You often hear people say that Jesus trained His 12 disciples by being with Him night and day for three years before He sent them out. However, a closer examination reveals that this is simply not the case. One of the first things He did after He called them was to send them out doing ministry on their own to do things like heal people, cast out demons, raise the dead, and proclaim the Kingdom of God all to places where Jesus had not even gone yet (Mark 6:7-13). These are aspects of ministry that we reserve for the most highly trained people and even then they're often perplexed. The best trained missionaries who have gone through years of seminary get into situations like that and often don't know what to do because they have not been on the bicycle. They've been watching the Tour de France on television in their training. They get out into the field and can't deal with these things that Jesus sent His disciples out to do as soon as He called them.

God worked through Peter as a cross-cultural worker (Acts 10:1-48). Speaking frankly, some might venture that this is a crazy idea. He was so ethnocentric that even when God gave him the vision of the unclean animals three times and told him to eat them, he refused God. So God had to intervene with a direct message. But even then,

Peter **still** hesitated before being willing to share his faith. Yet God used him to cross the divide between Jew and Gentile – to help launch the Gentile church.

When people obey and share what they have seen and heard from the Lord, they can overcome a huge lack of knowledge or training. The Holy Spirit in the lives of believers can be trusted. He is enough. What's more, when people **do** make mistakes, He can get over it. You remember the Sanhedrin marveled at the disciples in their power and their teaching because they were untrained (Acts 4:13). The popular characterization of highly-trained people is that they are arrogant. Paul wrote that "knowledge puffs up." Love is what matters — not knowledge.

God can use people who have remarkably little knowledge if they are faithful in sharing what He has done and what He has shown. In fact, it's often the most highly-trained, highly-educated and highly-gifted speakers who cast criticism on those who are untrained. They dishonor and disrespect those who do not have training. That sort of arrogance and disunity are exactly the kind of thing that the Lord opposes. God opposes the proud but gives grace to the humble. In Jesus's high priestly prayer in John 17, He focused so heavily on unity. Let us never disrespect other believers because they have less training. When we do this, we might indeed have great knowledge, but perhaps we don't share it as often with the unreached. What if a person with less knowledge shares more of his knowledge with the unreached than we do, even though his knowledge is less? When we gossip about others, we are not demonstrating the fruit of the Spirit: love, joy, peace, patience, kindness, goodness, faithfulness, gentleness, self-control (Galatians 5:22-23). Rather we are demonstrating the fruit of the flesh: pride, arrogance,

Photo 51: God opposes the proud but gives grace to the humble.

boastfulness, covetousness, and anger. In fact, we are demonstrating through our betrayal the fact that knowledge alone is not enough.

Lessons from the Apostle Paul

The apostle Paul normally demonstrated a very open and trusting approach. Sure, there were times when he made mistakes. But normally, he would go into a new city or town, lead people to the Lord and immediately engage them in ministry. He did that in different ways on different journeys as he learned better how to apply these principles. On his first journey he would quickly go into a place, lead people to the Lord, and then move on to the next place. On follow-up visits, he usually appointed elders and set them over the ministry in that local place. This system worked well for Paul. In fact, on subsequent journeys, sometimes new workers accompanied him from those same cities to new ministry sites. Meanwhile, works in former cities continued to grow in his absence. On still other journeys, he would try going from place to place, leaving a coworker behind in each location – workers like Luke, Timothy, and Silas. This worked okay too, except by the time he got to Athens, he was out of workers. He seemed to realize this wasn't such a good approach after all. So he continued to adapt. The reason it wasn't a good approach was because he realized that team ministry was more effective. So he went on to Corinth and waited for the team to re-gather and began a new approach where he stayed in one place a bit longer and, with the team, he trained people. Still, he was immediately engaging them in ministry as we can readily discern from reading the books of First and Second Corinthians. The third trip he focused mainly on Ephesus.

Some have pointed out that he trained for two years in the school of Tyrannus but we have to look at the big picture. At the end of those 2 years, it was said that already, every person in the Roman province of Asia had heard the gospel (Acts 19:8-10). For that to have happened, he positively had to be raising up members who went out immediately, then trained others. During this time, we know that Epaphras plants the church in Colossae and Hierapolis (Colossians 1:1-8, 4:12-13). We don't know the names of those who planted other churches in cities like Smyrna, Pergamum, Thyatira, Sardis, Philadelphia, and Laodicea. So the only conclusion we can draw is that Paul was training people in very short-term stints, then immediately sending them out for ministry. He could not have trained them for very long, because by the end of those two years, a huge impact had already been made.

Another problem with an approach that uses a long focused time of training is that teachers can give the impression that students have finished their training. That is never true. We need to develop disciples who realize that becoming a disciple is a lifetime process. If we set some arbitrary length of study as being significant it just tempts people to feel pride in finishing, followed by a sense of apathy in view of everything they've achieved. We see this over and over in people who go through long-term, high-level theological training. Some have observed that, of those who endure this type of training, few actually continue in ministry. That's a very difficult thing to overcome because we are training people in the hopes that they will **become** faithful rather than training them because they **have been** faithful (with what they had already received). You see one of the principles behind DMM/CPM is that we focus most heavily in training and coaching those who are faithful with what they've been given. Other models take people who say they want to be trained (who **say** they're faithful), then give them this huge amount of training. After all that, we hope they actually **are** faithful to apply and pass on what they've received. Unfortunately we're only creating a situation of more serious judgment for them because "from those to whom much has been given much shall be required" (Luke 12:48).

Discerning the Guidance of the Holy Spirit

God has specific desires for each of us. Scripture tells us that we are His workmanship created in Christ Jesus for good works which God prepared beforehand for us to walk in them (Ephesians 2:10). These specific desires that He has for us cannot be discerned simply from Scripture. We need to also be able to hear His voice and sense His leadership. And when we think we're hearing His voice, we need to know how to determine if it really is His voice (mainly by knowing how to compare our specific promptings to the general teachings in Scripture). Once we have verified our promptings with Scripture and we have made sure they are consistent with God's Word, then we need to obey what He tells us to do. Jesus talks repeatedly about how He only does what He sees the Father doing and He only says what He hears the Father saying (John 5:19, 6:38, 8:28). He tells the Pharisees the reason you do not hear God is because you do not belong to Him (John 8:47). The clear implication is that everyone who belongs to God can hear Him. In John 16, Jesus makes a big point of the fact that the function of the Holy Spirit is to speak the word of the Lord to us, to show the works of the Lord to us, so that we can know what He is desiring for us.

Jesus says, "My sheep listen to my voice; I know them, and they follow me" (John 10:27). We must teach people to recognize the voice of the Lord and respond to it. This is one key element to following Him. Being a disciple means being a follower. And you cannot follow someone if you cannot hear them or see them. You can know what they have said and you can believe it entirely but you cannot follow them unless you can hear them or see them. In intensive, long-term training programs, it is sometimes possible to become so focused on learning content that we fail to apply that content to our personal lives. We are so focused on preparing for a test, we forget to look in the mirror for the

Photo 52: Being a disciple means being a follower.

biggest test of all. We forget to apply the content to our own lives. This is a tragedy and the ironic thing is that it can be caused by being flooded with too much content.

Biblically, there are clear examples of Disciples who picked up even cross-cultural ministry fairly quickly. We already mentioned the Ethiopian treasurer (Acts 8:26-40). And what about all the believers who left Jerusalem because of the persecution (Acts 8:1)? They were scattered and when the church was scattered they began sharing wherever they went including with Gentiles. They didn't have a specific cross-cultural training. God used them despite their lack of training.

Interestingly, even in regard to knowledge new believers can learn remarkably quickly if they're using the approaches that movement principles suggest. I remember in China, in the first semester of a school year, several students became followers of Christ. They came from atheist backgrounds. They began using discipling patterns found in movement approaches. In the second semester they joined together for a retreat. In that retreat they were given a series of 700 Bible trivia questions and allowed to work together to try to answer those questions. They missed only two out of the 700. They had all been believers for less than six months. Because they were using these approaches they had grown that quickly in their knowledge of Scripture.

The Upside-Down Kingdom

When Jesus was born the angels did not announce it to the religious leaders or the political leaders. They announced the Good News to the shepherds and they, in turn, were faithful to tell others (Luke 2:8-20). Thus even in the birth of Christ, God foreshadowed His upside-down kingdom. His kingdom would be led by someone who did not have earthly power. His greatest victory would be won in the death of Jesus. He would use the weak and the despised things to shame the wise and the powerful. Yet somehow we still think that gaining academic prowess and respect are the keys to spreading the kingdom of God.

At the end of the Sermon on the Mount Jesus talks about the two foundations: the house built on the rock and the house built on the sand (Matthew 7:24-27). The difference was obedience. Obedience-based discipleship is biblical. We see the same idea in James when James talks about some people looking into the Word and not doing it versus those who look into the Word and they see themselves and they act accordingly by obeying (James 1:23-27).

Jesus's harshest judgment was on the best trained because they didn't obey what they knew. In the parable of the two sons it becomes clear that it's not people who talk a good game who are accepted but those who obey (Matthew 21:28-32). In the parable of the landowner we see that the tenants who do the will of the landowner are the ones who are accepted (Matthew 21:33-46). Knowledge only heaps up judgment if it's not obeyed. Therefore just-in-time training approaches are the natural and responsible way to deliver training.

Jesus said it wasn't the people who said to Him, "Lord, Lord," who will enter the kingdom but "those who do the will of my Father" (Matthew 7:21). It doesn't matter if you're doing miracles and doing ministry in the name of the Lord if you're not doing His will. The parable of the sheep and the goats illustrates this quite clearly (Matthew 25:31-46). We're not talking about earning salvation. Grace invalidates earning. But it does not invalidate effort. In fact it inspires effort. We are saved to serve. As the disciples said to the Sanhedrin, "We cannot but tell what we have seen and heard" (Acts 4:20). This needs to be imprinted upon every believer from the moment they come to faith.

In the Great Commission Jesus tells us what's involved in making disciples. They are to be baptized in the name of the Father and Son and Holy Spirit and they are to be taught to obey all that Christ commanded. That includes sharing with others and making disciples because He's just commanded them to do that. So often, people summarize the commands of Christ. We will teach outlines rather than what he actually commanded. It's instructive to make a list of the commands of Christ. It's a fairly subjective process to go through because you have to make some decisions about what you do with repetitive commands, what do you do with similar commands, which commands are intended to be for specific situations rather than general and so on. My list contains 94 commands and many of them are things that were never discussed as far as I can remember in my seminary education.

Of course, good and faithful people can come out of bad training practices. Gamaliel was evidently a man of faith (Acts 5:34, 22:3). This is despite the pharisaical system in which he was involved. Unfortunately, this tends to be the exception rather than the rule. I don't believe it's the fault of the people but largely the fault of the system which sets people up for failure in terms of how God works. Our training patterns do not parallel God's training patterns.

One thing that often happens to people who have received long-term intensive training is that they seem to be prone to making specific comparisons. They often think they are better than the person next to them, much like the Pharisee and the tax-collector (Luke 18:9-14). The Pharisee thanked the Lord that he was not a sinner like the tax-collector beside him. Meanwhile, the tax collector, beating his breast, did not dare even lift his eyes to heaven but said, "God have mercy on me, a sinner." And yet it was this tax collector who was right with God. We tend to train anyone that has the money, time, and desire versus training the humble, the faithful, and those with a learner mentality.

Heavy on the "Model-Assist"

We tend to heavily emphasize modeling with and assisting others. This can create dependency. Then, once people finish our formal intensive programs, we have very little ongoing coaching and accountability. The biblical patterns are quite the opposite. The biblical pattern is quickly model, provide only the essential early instruction, but then set up patterns of ongoing accountability within the church.

Sometimes, our church training approaches follow the lead of secular academics. In academia, every statement has to be supported by referencing what someone else has said and done. That is how we establish the truth and authority of our statements. We do this by referencing others. Jesus did not teach like this. Jesus did not teach like the

Photo 53: Jesus taught as one with authority. Our job is to follow.

scribes and Pharisees who taught in the same manner. In our formal trainings, we often spend far more time talking about what other people say about the Bible rather than simply studying the Bible. It's no wonder that we have people like the sons of Sceva who can talk about the God of Paul (Acts 19:11-20). But the demons did not recognize the sons of Sceva. Throughout the New Testament, demons always seemed to recognize Jesus (e.g., Mark 5:6-7). They recognized Paul. But they didn't recognize the sons of Sceva. Authority does not come from being able to footnote every statement. Authority comes from God and His Word. People who are following the Lord in the Holy Spirit can speak with great authority. Even children and uneducated people, after a short time, can learn to interpret and apply Scripture and become people of authority and power.

Our traditional approaches to training have a pre-determined pace. We have a school calendar as opposed to advancing to a new lesson only after a person has demonstrated his/her faithfulness. This is how God invests in us. It's far more important to develop people who are lifelong learners than people who have earned some sort of diploma.

Building faith and experience comes through investment. They are integrated into one's daily experience and interaction with others. This is an entirely different process than building knowledge into someone.

Licensing people produces theoreticians. Apprenticing people results in practitioners, implementers, and faithful people. These are people who reproduce. Actually, theoreticians reproduce also, but they tend to reproduce other theoreticians.

When we advance or recognize theoreticians, we're setting up a standard. We're suggesting that those are the people who have authority, that those are the individuals who have earned respect as opposed to advancing practitioners. I would suggest that, in the Kingdom of God, it is the practitioners who have earned the authority and respect. It is they who should be the standard. You do not achieve a standard like that by going through a set course. That happens only through living out and actively passing on what you have received. We tend to honor the people who have the highest degrees, the smoothest speakers, the winsome personalities, the most popular writers, and those who can woo the most followers from other people. This is one reason why 96 percent of church growth in the United States is transfer growth. We've become a church that follows celebrities. Instead, we should honor those who are the most faithful, those who demonstrate godly character, the humble, the loving, the fruitful, those who reproduce in others, serving and honoring others rather than being honored themselves.

We often tend to pull people out of their context to train them instead of training them in their own context. If we truly believe that this life of discipleship is for everyone, we cannot continue to do that because this means training is for a select few. We need everyone to be involved. Every member is a minister. Scripturally speaking, this means we are all priests. We are a kingdom of priests. We must be a people who are all equipped to minister not simply to be led by those who are paid to do so.

We've developed a culture of professionalism in the church which has sidelined the vast majority of people. We've become a garden full of beautiful hybrid plants that cannot reproduce rather than the tried and proven heirloom varieties that may not be so beautiful to look at but can reproduce generation after generation. We have developed a celebrity-leader culture versus a servant-leader culture. We have given far too much emphasis to individuals who have well-known names and charge big speaking fees versus people who leave a trail of faithful generational growth by serving others and leading from the background. Our Christian culture does not seem to reflect the kingdom culture.

Conclusion

Based on the fact that we haven't yet completed even a very basic version of the Great Commission (i.e., we haven't told the whole world the Good News for the first time), we can make an effective argument that the church needs a revised strategy for preparing workers. The way we've **been** doing training has not allowed us to finish the task. We can also make a very strong assertion that merely tweaking the length of training will not fix it. Whether it's three years or nine months, it still won't matter – because it's not just about time. The format itself hasn't served the appointed purpose for our intended result. Improving the content, in and of itself, is also insufficient. We can't just adjust the **amount** or the **nature** of the content. No specific content will be sufficient if it's divorced from a consistent link to **applying** that content and **passing it on** to others as an ongoing lifestyle. If we keep on doing exactly what we've been doing, we can only guess that we will keep getting the same result. To presume anything else would be nothing short of insanity. We need to look back at the New Testament and recover the biblical model for training new disciples. This book, these life practices, and these strategies are an attempt to do just that. May God bless our efforts to implement them for His glory and the advance of His Kingdom.

Photo 54: We need to look back at the New Testament and recover the biblical model for training new disciples.

Questions for Discussion:

1. Curtis Sergeant feels that two ideas have caused a number of problems in the church today. Which do you think has caused more problems than the other and why?

2. Does it bother you to consider that you might be following someone who is still "learning to ride a bike?" (In other words, could you see yourself following an imperfect mentor?) Explain your answer.

3. There have been some disturbing studies recently, like the one referenced in this chapter by Lifeway Research. Can you remember any recent findings about Christendom that shocked you? For example, something about a certain generation falling away or a study about how many people can't remember what the Great Commission is? How can you reconcile these findings with our current method of discipling believers? In other words, what has gone wrong? How would you fix things if you were in charge?

4. Where are you on the spectrum of knowledge versus practice? For example, do you believe God can work through a new believer to win or teach others? Why or why not?

5. This chapter emphasizes a humble spirit for all teachers. Can you remember a preacher or pastor who seemed a bit prideful? How did it impact your willingness to listen and obey?

WRAPPING UP

Questions for Discussion about the book as a whole:

1. What did you find most interesting in this book? What did you like?
2. What did you find most difficult? What caused you the most confusion?
3. What did you learn about people in this book?
4. What did this book teach you about God?
5. Is there anything in this book that you feel called to obey? What will you do about the things you've learned? What will be your next step? How will you begin implementing these teachings? Explain.
6. Is there someone you might be able to train about any of these concepts? (Please write down a name.) Who can you tell that might hold you accountable to do that?
7. With whom can you share this book and these teachings?

APPENDIX

Three-Thirds Group Guidesheet

Here is the entire guide for facilitating a three-thirds group in the style we teach:

Simple Group / Three-Thirds Process

Worship (5 min) – Use this time for praise and worship, and/or communion.

First: Look Back – 1/3 of your time (20 minutes)

Care – Share a story about how God revealed Himself to you or someone you know in an unexpected way. Or share with the group about your relationship with God during this past week. Or share a prayer request, an answer to prayer, etc. Pray for one another.

Loving Accountability. Review the prior lesson.

Please respond to the following questions:

1. How have you obeyed something that you learned from the prior lesson?
2. Who have you trained in something that you have learned?
3. With whom have you shared your story and/or God's story?
4. Who has believed?

Vision Casting - Share a story from the Bible (use one of the following Bible passages: Matt. 28:18-20, Luke 10:1-11, Acts 1:8, Luke 19:1-10, Matt. 13: 1-23, Luke 24:4549), or share an encouraging or inspirational story.

Next: Look Up– 1/3 of your time (20 minutes)
New Lesson. Pray & ask God to teach you this week's passage.

Read and discuss. Read this week's passage. Each person should respond to the questions:

1. What did you like about this passage?
2. What did you find difficult about this passage or what didn't you understand?

Reread this week's passage. Each person should respond to the questions:

1. What does this passage teach you about people?
2. What does this passage teach you about God/Jesus?

Then: Look Forward – 1/3 of your time (20 minutes)
Obey. Train. Share. - Everyone should pray for the Holy Spirit to show them how to answer these questions, then make commitments. Write down commitments.

1. How will you obey this passage?
2. Who will you train with this message?
3. With whom will you share your story or the story of God?

Practice.

In groups of two or three, practice what you have committed to do in question 5, 6 and 7. For example: role-play by practicing and teaching today's passage, or sharing the gospel/God's Story, or your personal testimony, etc.

Talk With God. In groups of two or three, pray for every member individually. Ask God to prepare the hearts of the people who will be hearing about Jesus this week. Ask Him to give you the strength to be obedient to your commitments.

Zúme Course Facilitator Guidesheet and Resources

Group Facilitator's Ministry Description

Zúme aims to equip and empower ordinary believers to reach every neighborhood. Zúme means yeast in Greek. In Matthew 13:33 Jesus is quoted as saying, "The Kingdom of Heaven is like a woman who took yeast and mixed it into a large amount of flour until it was all leavened." This illustrates how ordinary people, using ordinary resources, can have an extraordinary impact for the Kingdom of God.

Zúme training consists of ten two-hour sessions and includes:

- Video and audio to help your group understand basic principles of multiplying disciples.
- Group discussions to help your group think through what's being shared.
- Simple exercises to help your group put what you're learning into practice.
- Session challenges to help your group keep learning and growing between sessions.
- Session 10 is helpful once a person has started multiplying groups. For more frequently asked questions (FAQs), visit the Zúme website.

Serving as a facilitator for a Zúme group isn't rocket science, but nor is it completely intuitive either. Please consider and pray over these responsibilities and ask God to help you fulfill them in your next group.

A Zúme Facilitator should...

- Pray fervently for help from God in fulfilling these ministry objectives for the growth of God's Kingdom.
- Seek input from an experienced facilitator, if at all possible, and remain coachable throughout the experience.

- Gather a group of 4-11 other people (12 maximum, including yourself) then make sure they all register as a participant in your group at www.zúmeproject.com. Get their email addresses and cell phone numbers so you can contact them. You might also consider using an app like Podio or a private Facebook group to communicate. There are dozens of apps you can consider. Take your pick. Choose a favorite.

- Get to know your group members personally as soon as possible.

- Make sure everyone in your group knows when, where, and for how long you're meeting. It will take approximately two full hours to do each session. Groups of 6 or less might finish in 90 minutes on some nights. The course can't easily be cut into one-hour segments.

- Try to set the meeting place in a location that is somewhat close to an area of town with at least some level of foot traffic. Meeting in a remote location or a building out in the country might be beautiful for enjoying God's creation, but it won't help much when it comes time to prayer walk among people.

- Arrive early enough to work out the tech challenges (or visit the site in advance). You'll need a way to project or view the Zúme session videos so the text on the screen is big enough for everyone in the group to read. If you plan to connect a laptop to a flat-screen TV, you might need an HDMI cable. If you're simply going to use a tablet or laptop, you'll at least need access to Wi-Fi (until sessions are made to be downloadable, which might indeed happen at some point in the future). If you're not tech-savvy, find someone to help you.

- Always start and end on time. Look through the session in advance to plan your pacing. Also, be sure to note if there are any special materials needed on any special evenings (e.g., material for Lord's supper, pens/pencils, or even pictures of public places [if you need to provide them for the night you prayer walk]).

- Optional: Would your group members like to organize snacks/ refreshments? Help them determine a schedule. But help them remember that refreshments can't become so central that they rob time from the session itself. At most, allow 10 or 15 minutes sometime in the middle for a refreshment/rest room break.
- In general, your role is to make sure everyone has a chance to ask/answer questions and participate. Don't permit disrespectful behavior.
- One of the most important roles of the facilitator is to keep the value of multiplication before the group at all times. At least once in every session, try to find an appropriate place to remind the group that in session 9, group members will be given a chance to share their plans (their calling) for next steps. Let them know repeatedly that the goal of Zúme is to become a disciple worth multiplying then to obey. Help them imagine what it might be like to start their own group or help someone else begin one. Begin watching for group members who mention a willingness to tackle this after the first 9 sessions are done – and if anyone mentions a desire to do so, encourage them and ask if they have questions or need help figuring out how to make it happen. Constantly think about your own actions to make sure they are easily reproducible. For example, we recommend you not volunteer to buy everyone a coffee at each night's meeting because group members might not be able to afford to do so. They might be embarrassed about it and might avoid starting a new group because they assume every good facilitator should do so.
- Remember you're trying to learn to be like Jesus. Jesus noticed the people around him. He reached out to their needs. If you have a personality that doesn't normally focus on the needs of others around you, try to make a conscious effort to up your game in this area. None of us will be a perfect facilitator – but relational networking was a specialty of Jesus, and it should be for us too.

- When you get to session 9, it's so much easier if the group fills out the goal sheet (their hopeful plans) online. For that, they'll need to be logged in with their own credential. For this reason, try to help them get logged in from the start and become accustomed to accessing Zúme webpages. They'll likely need to do so anyway, if they start a new group themselves. (If they use the online page, all the pages are available for you to review digitally and they're archived on the site.)
- The most important outcome of Zúme is to become a disciple worth multiplying then to start new groups. Make sure you help them understand that in session 9. They don't have to fill out every blank. But make sure they give priority, at least, either to launching a new Zúme group or a three-thirds group or **both**. Remember that they can be "members of two groups." They could keep a regular three-thirds group going for their own "spiritual group" – and start a 3/3 group or another Zúme for outreach. (We wish every believer would do exactly that. Multiplying Zúme groups is great. But 3/3 groups are much more likely to become a permanent "spiritual family" than 10-week Zúme groups alone.)
- Session 10 will be helpful once the group member has started a new generation (or two). Still, we recommend that Zúme groups include it, even with newcomers, since they'll need this knowledge later anyway.
- The sixth session is unique. It contains the only video of any size – the only video longer than 10 minutes in the entire course. Some might feel more comfortable if they know that session 6 is different. In some groups, we ask them to watch the session 6 video in advance, when they feel totally awake and rested. In other cases, we've told them to bring some coffee and make sure they've gotten plenty of sleep the night before. (The main video in session 6 is a full-length model of a three-thirds group. It's extremely important. Never skip it. By seeing that model,

they know what to strive for.) Just be ready to rev up your group. Make sure they know of the session's importance as a good model.

- One of the key roles you serve is to cast vision for the group. Remember – the vision is to become a disciple worth multiplying then to multiply groups. The benchmark for measuring whether or not your group was successful won't be known until the week or two after you wrap up. Why? Because the goal is to become a disciple worth multiplying then to multiply groups. **Thanks for your shared vision and partnership!**

Sample Shema Statements

One of the hardest parts about doing DMM is getting from "Hello" to a spiritual conversation or group. Statements like these (below) can help you divert the subject toward spiritual things and even "filter" to see if your friend or listener is open to hearing spiritual things. Some call these "Shema" statements. (Shema is the Aramaic word for "Listen.") In addition, statements like these can help others realize that you are a genuinely a person of faith. As a result, if/when they have a problem or feel troubled someday, they might come to you seeking spiritual help. If they have a spiritual dream, for example, or if they feel at the end of their rope, they might ask for guidance. Of course, these statements only work if you're truly authentic from the inside out in your love and speech. On top of all that, they help us establish more courage in bringing up God in our everyday conversations. Try setting a goal to use one Shema statement per day.

- "I read something that seems hard for me to obey in the Bible today".
- "I wonder how _____(a religious behavior) connects to _____ (a heart issue)?"
- Verbally long for the day when ugly things will be swept away when Jesus returns.
- "God speaks to me in prayer or through his Word."
- "I was having a hard time with _____ (an issue), so I _____ (a spiritual solution)."
- "I asked God for help and He..."
- Ask questions like, "How do you show love to God?" or "What was the last thing you heard from God?"
- "I read a wonderful story today. May I tell you?"
- "God taught me something today."
- "I read something really interesting about God today."
- "God is light, and he shines into the dark places of my heart."
- "Do you think God could stop all of the bloodshed in...?"

- "Did you ever have a dream from God?"
- Use a Proverb to apply to a current situation.
- "How should a person of God act here?"
- Thank God for something difficult.
- "Do you think God cares about....?"
- "God wants to walk with me so I walk with Him."
- "I believe only with God there is hope for...."
- When telling your children's names, or your own name, share the meaning.
- Mention something that you prayed for and how it was answered.
- Response to a social issue.
- "Jesus dealt with _____ and said some interesting things about it."
- "As I was praying for you today I sensed God..."
- "I feel encouraged about something that I learned about God."
- If you are by the sand or looking at stars in the sky, reminisce about God's blessing to Abraham.
- "God healed my friend."
- "I feel sad when I see trash, because God created the earth."
- "I was reading today and God reminded me..."
- "I am thankful for _____. What are you thankful for?"
- "God hates injustice and he has a lot to say about it."
- "Do you know which day God created...?"
- Context = complaining about their country... "It doesn't matter which country you are in but to be where God wants you to be." "I know this is a place of great conflict and God wants you to experience peace."
- "Can I tell you a story?"
- "I don't need _____ to protect me. I pray for God to protect me."
- Children: "Blessing and hard work make me rely more on God."

- Spouse: "God will give me a wife in just the right time."
- In response to not having children... "Marriage is a picture of Jesus and His church."
- "Yes, I miss home, but God meets me in my loneliness. God will never leave me nor forsake me.
- "What is most important to you?"
- "What do you think are the most important values you can give to your children?"
- "When did you feel most safe or secure?"
- "Can we pray for this meal?"
- "Can we please bless your home or your family?"

(These sample statements adapted from the list accessed at https://www.jeannie-marie.com/articles-and-resources/2017/11/fifteen-shema-statements-you-can-say on April 10, 2019.)

Go Deeper

To learn more about CPM/DMM principles, strategies and life practices, visit

www.MoreDisciples.com

where we will post improvements and revisions to this book, along with dozens more helpful resources.

GLOSSARY

3/3 Group = See three-thirds group.

Accountability Groups = Meetings staged between two or three people of the same gender - men with men, women with women - once a week to pray and discuss a set of questions that help reveal areas where things are going right and other areas that need correction.

CMM = Church multiplication movement = See CPM. (For the purposes of this book, we are defining CMM and DMM to be synonymous.)

CPM = Church-planting movement = A rapid multiplication of indigenous churches planting churches that sweeps through a people group or population segment

Disciple = a follower of Christ who hears, obeys, and shares the Good News with others, then trains them to do the same. Put another way, a disciple loves God, loves people, and makes other disciples.

Discovery Bible Study = (See Three-Thirds group)

DMM (Disciple-making movement) = See CPM. (For the purposes of this book, we are defining CPM and DMM to be synonymous.)

Three-thirds group = A 3/3 group, then, is a gathering of 4-12 people who want to learn to love God, love others, and make disciples. They "do life" together in their 3/3 group, holding one another accountable to goals that they, themselves, set, in response to hearing God's Word and applying it. The name comes from the fact that the study consists of three "thirds" – a look back (at the past week), a look up (at what God has said in a portion of His Word), and a look forward (at goals for the coming week). A 3/3 group essentially can be a "simple church," either standing on its own, or within the context of a larger "city church" or "regional church network."

Zúme = A web-driven training experience with 10 sessions focused on becoming a disciple worth multiplying. It also teaches personal and group-oriented CPM/DMM strategies to share our faith and grow the church.

REFERENCES

24:14. (2018). *History*. Retrieved from https://www.2414now.net/history

2414. (2018, 10 22). *Frequently Asked Questions*. Retrieved from 2414: https://www.2414now.net/faqs

Allen, R. (1962). *The Spontaneous Expansion of the Church*. Grand Rapids: Wm. B. Eerdmans Publishing Company.

Billy Graham Center. (2018, 10 22). *Archives*. Retrieved from Billy Graham Center: https://www2.wheaton.edu/bgc/archives/guides/046.htm

Bosch, D. J. (2001). *Transforming Mission: Paradigm Shifts in Theology of Mission*. Maryknoll, New York: Orbis Books.

Brame, C. J. (n.d.). *Center for Teaching*. Retrieved from https://www.vanderbilt.edu: https://cft.vanderbilt.edu/wp-content/uploads/sites/59/Active-Learning.pdf

Campbell, F. (2016, February 29). *Mission Frontiers*. Retrieved from http://www.missionfrontiers.org/issue/article/gospel-tool

Cheney, C. (2018, Aug 13). *Devex*. Retrieved from Is the world more urban than UN estimates? It depends on the definition: https://www.devex.com/news/is-the-world-more-urban-than-un-estimates-it-depends-on-the-definition-93175

Cole, N. (2010). *Church 3.0: Upgrades for the Future of the Church*. San Francisco: Jossey-Bass.

Eims, L. (1978). *The Lost Art of Disciple Making*. Grand Rapids: Zondervan.

Freeman, S. E. (2014). Active learning increases student performance in science, engineering, and mathematics. *Proceedings from the National Academy of Sciences USA 111*, 8410-8415.

Freeman, S. E. (2014). *Proceedings from the National Academy of Sciences USA 111, 8410-8415*. Retrieved from Active learning increases student performance in science, engineering, and mathematics: http://www.pnas.org/content/pnas/111/23/8410.full.pdf

Garrison, D. (2004). *Church Planting Movements*. Richmond, VA: WIGTake Resources.

Garrison, D. (2014). *A Wind in the House of Islam*. Monument, CO: WIGTake Resources.

International Bulletin of Missionary Research. (1979, January). Retrieved from The Legacy of R. Kenneth Strachan: http://www.internationalbulletin.org/issues/1979-01/1979-01-002-roberts.pdf

Jordan, W. (2015, February 12). Retrieved from YouGov.co.uk: https://yougov.co.uk/news/2015/02/12/third-british-adults-dont-believe-higher-power/)

Lausanne Movement. (2018, 10 22). *The Legacy of the Lausanne Movement*. Retrieved from The Lausanne Movement: https://www.lausanne.org/our-legacy

Lucas, D. and Patterson, G. (2017). "The Magic of Multiplication" (2017, April 27), Retrieved from http://www.moredisciples.com/webinars.

McGavran, D. (1975). *Bridges of God*. United Kingdom: World Dominion Press.

McGavran, D. (1976). *Understanding Church Growth*. USA: William B. Eerdsman Publishing Company.

Millar, F. (2006). *A Greek Roman Empire: Power and Belief under Theodosius II (408-450)*. University of California Press Books.

O'Brien, W., & Parks, K. (2018, Jan 1). *Mission Frontiers*. Retrieved from Why is 24:14 different than previous efforts? : http://www.missionfrontiers.org/issue/article/why-is-2414-different-than-previous-efforts

Patterson, G. (1976). Obedience-Oriented Education. Portland, OR: Author.

Piper, J. (2010). *Let the Nations be Glad*. Retrieved from www.desiringgod.org: https://document.desiringgod.org/let-the-nations-be-glad-pdf-excerpt-en.pdf?ts=1446647796

Project, Z. (n.d.). *Session 2*. Retrieved from Producers and Consumers video script: www.ZumeProject.com

Reach, R. M. (2016). *Movements that Move*. St. Charles, IL: ChurchSmart Resources.

Ridout, S. (2018, October 31). *GACX*. Retrieved from A Global Alliance for Church Multiplication: https://gacx.io/articles/nine-questions-for-healthy-movements/

Sergeant, C. (2015, November 23). Retrieved from YouTube: https://www.youtube.com/watch?v=s-fnImBNckU

Sergeant, C. (2018, 10 22). *Multiplication Concepts*. Retrieved from Every Marine a Rifleman: https://www.youtube.com/watch?v=s-fnImBNckU

Sergeant, C. (2018, May 1). The Zume Project Igniting The Spark. *Mission Frontiers*, pp. 6-11.

Shank, N., & Shank, K. (n.d.). *Four fields of kingdom growth*. Retrieved from https://static1.squarespace.com/static/588ada483a0411af1a-b3e7ca/t/58a40ef11b631bcbd49c88c0/1487146760589/4-Fields-Nathan-Shank-2014.pdf

Smietana, B. (2016, September 27). *Americans Love God and the Bible, Are Fuzzy on the Details*. Retrieved from Lifeway: https://lifewayresearch.com/2016/09/27/americans-love-god-and-the-bible-are-fuzzy-on-the-details

Smith, B. (2018, 10 11). The Truth about Movements. (D. Lucas, Interviewer) London, England.

Smith, S., & Kai, Y. (2011). *T4T: A Discipleship Re-Revolution*. WIGTake Resources.

Team Expansion. (2018). Retrieved from 3 Circles: https://vimeo.com/289340874

Treadgold, W. (1997). *A History of the Byzantine State and Society.* Stanford University Press.

Trousdale, J. (2018). *The Kingdom Unleashed.* Murfreesboro, TN: DMM Library.

ZumeProject. (2018). Retrieved from http://www.zumeproject.com

ZumeProject. (n.d.). *Session 1.* Retrieved from SOAPS video script: https://www.ZumeProject.com

ZumeProject. (n.d.). *Session 1.* Retrieved from Accountability Groups: https://www.ZumeProject.com

ZumeProject. (n.d.). *Session 1.* Retrieved from Welcome to Zume video script: https://www.ZumeProject.com

ZumeProject. (n.d.). *Session 2.* Retrieved from Producers and Consumers video script: www.ZumeProject.com

ZumeProject. (n.d.). *Session 2.* Retrieved from The Prayer Cycle: https://www.ZumeProject.com

ZumeProject. (n.d.). *Session 3.* Retrieved from Spiritual Breathing video script: https://www.ZumeProject.com

ZumeProject. (n.d.). *Session 5.* Retrieved from Prayer Walking: https://www.ZumeProject.com

ZumeProject. (n.d.). *Session 9.* Retrieved from Part of Two Churches video script: https://www.ZumeProject.com

TABLE OF FIGURES

ABOUT THE AUTHORS

David Garrison serves as Church Planting Consultant with Missio Nexus and is Executive Director of Global Gates (GlobalGates. info), a recruiting, coaching, and training organization based in New York, New York. He has a PhD in historical theology and is a veteran of more than 30 years as a missionary pioneer. He wrote *The Nonresidential Missionary* (1990), *Church Planting Movements* (2004), and *A Wind in the House of Islam* (2014).

Doug Lucas is founder and President of Team Expansion (Team-Expansion.org). He has led teams in Uruguay and also in the USSR (Ukraine), where God raised up the beginnings of a church-planting movement. He has a Masters Degree in Missions, along with an MBA and a Doctorate in Business Administration. Since 1995, he has edited Brigada, a weekly missions e-zine (brigada.org). He is married to Penny and they have two adult children, Chris and Caleb.

Curtis Sergeant served as a missionary on a large island off the coast of China from 1991 to 2002. While there, they saw God increase the number of Disciples from 100 to over 500,000, primarily through multiplication of simple reproducible tools. Since 2015, he has led in developing the Zúme Project (ZúmeProject.com). He has a Doctorate in Missions and is the Founder of MetaCamp (metacamp.org).

INDEX

Note: Scripture passages are at the beginning of the index in alphabetical order (not the order of biblical books) and are preceded with an asterisk.